ECONOMICS FOR LIFE

101 Lessons You Can Use *Every Day!*

Bruce Madariaga
Montgomery College

Editor-in-Chief: George Hoffman
Senior Sponsoring Editor: Ann West
Marketing Manager: Mike Schenk

Printed in the U.S.A.

ISBN: 0-618-57641x

123456789-MP-09 08 07 06 05

BRIEF CONTENTS

CONTENTS

CHAPTER 4: Solve Riddles and Mysteries:

PREFACE

For The Economics User

This book may surprise you.

First, many people believe economics is about money and business and not much else. This book soundly debunks this belief. After reading this book you will learn that economics is virtually everywhere and applies to virtually everything. You will learn that lessons from economics can be used everyday throughout your life. Indeed, Professor Alfred Marshall had it right when he characterized economics as "The ordinary business of life."

Second, the field of economics is often stereotyped as technical, confusing, graphical, theoretical, impractical, dry, and boring. In fact, economics has come to be known as "the dismal science." Many books about economics reinforce this stereotype.

Economics for Life addresses these characterizations head on. Nothing technical is presented. Plain language, not mathematics or graphics, is used to explain economic ideas. Real world application is the theme of the book. And fascinating ideas, sprinkled with irony and surprise, are found throughout much of the book.

Finally, most books about learning economics start by teaching theoretical concepts and models. At best, these books attach a few applications of economic theory at the end of chapters or at the end of the book.

Economics for Life takes a different approach. This book starts with applications and ends with applications. Along the way you will learn key economic concepts, but not for the sake of learning them. Instead you will learn economics to help yourself understand the world and make better decisions throughout your life.

So get comfortable, start reading, and remember,

The real purpose of education is <u>not</u> knowledge. The real purpose of education is action!

Use what you learn.

For The Economics Instructor

"Students have unnecessary difficulty learning economics because textbooks generally do not have enough good examples of real-world applications."[1]

--Gary S. Becker
Nobel Laureate Professor of Economics

Economics for Life contains a large collection of real world applications, paradoxical results, critiques of common fallacies, and solutions to mysteries that are sure to interest students of economics. Students are shown how to use the economic concepts taught in microeconomic and macroeconomic principles classes to make better decisions and understand the world. By studying interesting and relevant applications of economic principles, students learn how economic knowledge and thinking can assist them throughout their lives.

Economics for Life also serves as a valuable resource for teaching economics. Instructors are offered a novel resource for helping them deliver a more applications-based economic principles course to provide a more relevant, interesting, and successful learning experience for their students.

While *Economics for Life* can be used by all students and instructors of economic principles, Appendix A1 makes this book particularly well suited as a supplement for students and instructors using Boyes/Melvin's *Economics* or *Fundamentals of Economics* textbooks, or John Taylor's *Economics* textbook. All three of these texts are published by Houghton Mifflin. Appendix A1 links lessons from this book to the associated chapters within these texts. Thus, instructors can easily assign read-

---

[1] "Not-so-dismal Scientist", Business Week, Oct. 21st, 1996, p.19.

ings from *Economics for Life* to supplement, reinforce, and bring to life reading assignments when using a Houghton Mifflin Principles of Economics text.

In Appendices A2 and A3, specific economic concepts and general lessons from economics are linked to the 101 lessons contained in the *Economics for Life*. Thus, when teaching a particular economic concept or general economic lesson, economics instructors can use this book as a reference for identifying applications, riddles, and mysteries, to illustrate the concept or general lesson, motivate classroom discussion, and/or identify interesting homework assignments.

As economic educators, we all know we must demonstrate relevance and ignite curiosity to motivate our students. Once students understand how they benefit from understanding economics and how interesting economics can be, they will want to learn more. Once they want to learn more, they will. My hope is this book will help you make this happen for your students.

About the Author

Once upon a time there was a young man who was an incurable schoolaphobic. No one could get him to attend school. Through ninth grade he was absent 60, 70, 80 plus days each year. At the end of ninth grade he dropped out and never attended high school. No one in his family had ever gone to college; why should he?

The local community college saved this young man from walking down a dead end path. He passed the GED (high school equivalency) test that was offered at this college. The college then invited this junior high dropout to attend college classes. He accepted the offer. One semester he took a class called "Principles of Economics," even though he had no idea what it was about. A light bulb flashed. He went on to spend many years studying economics at the University of Delaware, the University of Maryland, and finally at Harvard University. Yes, thanks to Delaware County Community College, this junior high dropout earned a graduate degree from Harvard.

One sunny day many years later he returned to Delaware County Community College—to give the commencement speech to the graduating class of year 2000. He told the graduates about his story, about how their community college had saved him, and about a class he once took called "Principles of Economics." Then, after 15 rewarding years in the U.S. government, this not-as-young man decided to leave his position as a senior economist and return to serve the community college system that had once saved him. Today he teaches economics with great passion and joy to students who are struggling with life like he was many years before.

PART ONE:
USING ECONOMICS TO MAKE BETTER DECISIONS

Introduction

Economics is sometimes defined as "the science of choice." It is largely about how to make smart decisions. Individuals, businesses, and governments have to make choices or decisions because their resources are scarce. For example, you have to choose how to spend your money, time, and energy because your money, time, and energy are limited or scarce. Learning economics will help you make these decisions wisely.

Economics teaches us how to think and make decisions logically and scientifically in order to make ourselves as well off as possible. Economic logic requires we take three basic steps when making any decision.

STEP 1: Weigh benefits against the costs.

STEP 2: Count only additional benefits and additional costs.

STEP 3: Be sure to count all additional benefits and additional costs.

These steps apply to any decision you will ever make. Master them and you will make better decisions throughout your life.

To illustrate how to take these steps, consider the following common real world business decision:

Should you videoconference or travel to a business meeting?

Suppose you own a profitable small business in Washington, D.C. You desire to hold an essential 1-hour meeting with business executives in New York, NY. You have two options:

1

a. You can fly to New York. You own 25,000 frequent-flyer miles, which you can return to the airline at any time for a free ticket anywhere in the United States. Thus, you need not pay for your flight to New York. Your only expenditures would be for 15-minute cab rides to and from the airport in D.C. (fare = $25 each way) plus 15-minute cab rides to and from the airport in New York (fare = $25 each way). Or,

b. You can use a video conferencing facility. Last January, you paid $3,000 to obtain access to a video conferencing facility located within your office building for one year. You also must pay $125/hour for each hour the facility is used.

You estimate the meeting will be equally effective if held in person or via video conferencing. (Meeting face to face has advantages, but video conferencing may impress the other executives.)

Which option should you choose? How should you think about this decision?

STEP 1: Since this meeting has been judged to be essential, it is reasonable to assume that the benefits of having the meeting exceed the costs. Thus, you should have the meeting. But the question at hand is, "Should you videoconference?" To make this decision, you must first compare the costs of videoconferencing with the benefits of videoconferencing. The costs of videoconferencing are discussed above. The only benefits of videoconferencing, given that the meeting would be equally effective via teleconference or travel, are the costs you would save by not having to travel. Thus, the decision of how to hold the meeting should depend on which option is less costly.

STEP 2: It is important to recognize that the $3,000 cost to obtain access to the conferencing facility is *not* an additional cost (or *marginal cost*) of using the conferencing facility for the purposes of holding this meeting. The $3,000 is what economists call a *sunk cost*. Sunk costs are irrelevant to decision making and should be ignored. They are history, like spilled milk. No sense crying over spilled milk; no sense letting sunk costs affect your decisions about the future. The fact that you already paid for access to the facility should neither encourage nor discourage you from using the facility today. The relevant question now is, "Are the marginal costs from travel to New York more or less than the marginal costs from teleconferencing?"

STEP 3: The marginal costs associated with travel are not entirely obvious. First, there are the cab fares ($25 × 4 = $100). If $100 was the only additional cost, option (a) would be less costly and preferred to option (b). But there are other costs associated with option (a). It takes more time to travel. Time costs are real costs. You could use the time it would take to travel to earn additional income or have fun. Also, you would lose a frequent flyer ticket by traveling. Just because you own the miles doesn't mean it is free to use them! By going to New York, you give up the opportunity to use the miles for some other trip. Thus, the true cost (or *opportunity cost*) of flying equals $100 + lost value of time + lost airline ticket. This cost undoubtedly exceeds the $125 marginal cost of videoconferencing. Thus, you should stay in D.C.

This example illustrates how economic thinking and key economic concepts such as marginal cost and opportunity cost can be used to make a practical decision. Part One of this book provides numerous examples of how you can apply economics to help you make better personal and business decisions throughout your life.

Finally, as you read the examples of using economics in this book, you will encounter various economic terms and concepts written in italics. You will learn the basic meaning of these terms and concepts by studying the various applications presented. However, each example is written concisely and focused on the application of economics rather than the underlying economic theory involved. Technical detail, exceptions to the norm, and theoretical underpinnings are not what this book is about. You may wish to learn more about the underlying economic principles used in the lessons that follow so that you will be better prepared to apply economics to applications unrelated to those in this book. The Appendix of *Economics for Life* may help you obtain a deeper understanding of these economic principles by linking the 101 lessons in this book to specific economic terms and concepts, general economic lessons, and economic textbook chapters.

CHAPTER 1:
Make Better Personal Decisions

Introduction

This chapter is about many of the most important decisions you will make during your lifetime. The purpose of this chapter is to provide you with valuable tips about how to make these decisions wisely. All of the advice provided follows from basic economic principles, such as the three steps to decision making discussed above. These same principles will apply, however, to many other smaller decisions you will encounter throughout your life. So learn these economic principles well and you will benefit in unpredictable ways.

Lastly, economic principles alone will rarely provide definitive answers. Rather, economics teaches a logical approach to decision making and provides numerous general tips that can be used to help you with your decisions. So let's start applying economics to analyze some big decisions.

1.   Attending College

The decision to attend college should be approached much like any other decision—by comparing benefits and costs. However, as is often the case with big decisions, the computation and proper comparison of the benefits and costs of attending college are not entirely simple.

What are your costs of attending college? Your obvious, explicit costs include tuition, fees, books, supplies, and transportation (no food and clothing costs unless these costs are higher because you attend college). But you may be surprised to learn that all of these costs are usually dwarfed by your implicit costs of attending college—the time and energy you give up by attending college. These implicit costs are real costs that should be considered when deciding to attend college. If instead of going to college you would spend your time and energy working full-time, then your full cost (or *opportunity cost*) of attending college includes the earnings you forego by not working. If instead of going to college you would spend your time and energy having fun, then your full opportunity cost of attending college includes the value of the fun you lost by spending your time in college classrooms. In any case, your true cost of attending college is likely to far exceed your tuition and other obvious costs of college.

What are your benefits of attending college? Educational attainment is highly correlated with lifetime earnings. For example, average lifetime earnings in the United States are roughly 75% greater for those with a bachelor's degree (approximately $2.1 million) compared with those with only a high school degree (approximately $1.2 million). College graduates who go on to earn graduate degrees achieve even greater earnings. Lifetime earnings for those that attain professional degrees such as lawyers and medical doctors are on average more than twice the lifetime earnings of those with just a bachelor's degree. Moreover, the earnings benefits from educational attainment have been steadily rising over time. So while your costs of attending college may be greater than you initially thought, so, too, might your benefits.

But extra income is not the only benefit of attending college. You may learn things (like economics) that may help you manage your everyday life. You may feel better about yourself after you attain educational goals. You may make many new friends. You may meet your future life partner! These outcomes are potentially large benefits of attending college and should not be ignored. The general lesson here is that when weighing the costs and benefits of a decision, be sure to include (at least qualitatively) all relevant non-monetary benefits and costs.

The comparison of the costs and benefits of attending college also entails complications. First, it is important to compare the additional (or *marginal*) costs with the additional (or *marginal*) benefits of attending college. For example, if you already have a degree, the additional benefits (at least in the form of future earnings) of completing another semester of course work may be small relative to the additional opportunity cost you would incur. But if you are one semester from attaining a degree, the additional benefits of staying in college another semester to get your degree may be large relative to the additional costs involved.

Second, going to college is an investment. While the costs of attending college occur today, the benefits from attending college occur throughout one's lifetime. Thus, the expected lifetime earnings benefits from educational attainment cited above are somewhat misleading because much of the extra earnings from completing college degrees would accrue many years into the future. Such future benefits should not be directly compared with the up-front costs of attending college. This is because benefits received in the future are not worth as much as benefits received today. For example, if another $1,000 investment in education today yielded only an extra $1,050 in income five years from now, you should not make the investment. You would be better off saving your $1,000 and accruing interest for five years. So, benefits (or costs) expected to accrue in the future must be *discounted* into *present value* terms before they are compared. [For example, if the interest rate you could receive on your savings equaled 5%, the present value of $1,050 five years from now would equal $1,050/(1 + 0.05)^5 = $823, which is less than a $1,000 present value cost.]

No general analysis can answer whether you should attend college and for how long. The benefits you would receive from a college experience depend in significant part on personal preferences and circumstances. But this lesson does provide a logical framework and some insights that can help you think through these important high-cost, high-benefit decisions.

2. Selecting a College

Economics provides a few insights regarding the choice of which college to attend. All else being equal, a college degree from a higher-rated college is more valuable than one from a lower-rated one. This seems obvious since we might expect that someone graduating from the more highly rated college would learn more. But this is probably not the primary reason why graduates from more elite colleges receive higher earnings. When hiring new workers, employers must attempt to evaluate applicants based on very incomplete information. They use an applicant's college achievement as a *signal* of an applicant's general capabilities. The employer may reason, for example, that an applicant who has managed to beat out fierce competition to get into Harvard, then beat out competition from talented Harvard students to pass difficult courses, probably has a lot on the ball and will be worth a high salary, *even if the applicant has not learned anything relevant to the job at hand.*

So, a college degree earned from a more highly ranked school is likely to yield greater lifetime earnings. (High grades also may increase the salary you receive in your first job after college, but employers rarely review grades thereafter.) This does not necessarily mean you should attend the most elite college you can get into. First, elite colleges tend to be more expensive. Second, benefits other than earnings potential, such as the benefits from the amenities, location, etc., from attending a college should be considered. Finally, what usually matters most to employers is the quality of the school associated with your last degree. For example, if you wish to attend a high-rated university, attending a 2-year community college first may still be a good strategy. If you are a strong student capable of attending an elite university, you would likely receive high grades at a community college and then be able to transfer after two years to an elite school. Meanwhile, you would save a lot on tuition and possibly room and board costs. Similarly, if you are destined for graduate school, your chances of getting into a highly rated graduate school may not depend significantly on the rating of the undergraduate college you attend (since you may receive higher grades by attending a lower rated undergraduate college). However, the additional or *marginal* benefits of a graduate degree may significantly depend on the rating of your undergraduate college. For example, the additional benefits of a graduate degree from Harvard would be greater if your undergraduate degree was from your local state college than if it was from Harvard (since you could already market the Harvard signal if you attended Harvard as an undergraduate).

To summarize, while many personal factors should influence your selection of a college, attending a highly regarded college, especially to complete your final degree, will send a valuable information signal to potential employers (as well as to other acquaintances) that will last throughout your lifetime.

3.   Working While in College

How much will your lifetime earnings increase if you decide to work while attending college? Answer: Possibly not at all. Indeed, your lifetime earnings may fall if you work significant hours while attending college. While your *opportunity cost* of attending college includes the lost earnings from not having as much time to work, your opportunity cost of working includes the delay in higher earnings that you will likely receive after completing college. Since the benefit of educational attainment, in terms of increased earnings, has increased dramatically in the United States over the last few decades, any delay in completing college is very costly. If working while in college means delaying graduation, then it is likely your employment will decrease, not increase your lifetime earnings. Moreover, if working while in college reduces your performance in college (you learn less and your grades suffer), you may reduce the value of your degree and your post-college earnings. Thus, if at all possible, it may be in your long-term interest to quit your low-paying job, complete your degree as quickly as possible (take additional credits, attend summer classes, etc.) without jeopardizing performance, and borrow your way through college.

One important exception to this recommendation is when your employment provides valuable experience or contacts. Accumulating such experience and personal connections may be worth delaying your graduation date. But if you are working a job to pay the bills that do not provide career benefits, you may be wise to go into debt.

4.   Selecting a Major and a Career

Your choice of career direction is critical to your long-term happiness. Like any other decision, your career choice should be based on a comparison of benefits and costs. A benefit you will no doubt wish to include in your calculations is expected earnings. But how do you know which occupations will provide higher incomes in the future?

In free market economies, earnings are determined by the forces of *supply* and *demand*. Occupations in high demand but where supply of workers is low command the highest salaries. Superstar athletes make a lot of money because the demand for their services is so high and the supply of superstars is so low.

To estimate the earnings potential of different occupations it is necessary to project future demand and supply. For example, given our aging population, demand for nurses will no doubt rise substantially over the next several decades. All else being equal, nursing salaries should rise. But eventually the prospects of higher salaries may induce more college students to major in nursing. A greater supply of nurses could reverse the positive effect on salaries from rising demand. Herein lies the rub. Unless for some reason labor supply is restricted, the high salaries caused by high demand will eventually attract more workers and this competition will drive salaries downward again. If so, then why do salaries of different occupations vary so much? The reason is because the supply of workers in many occupations is limited.

Consider dentistry. Why do dentists make high salaries year after year? They do so because the supply of dentists is limited. First, one must invest in a lot of education and hard work to become a dentist. Many people do not wish to make such an investment. This limits supply. Second, it takes a certain amount of natural skill and intelligence to become a dentist, which many people do not have. This limits supply. Third, many people might find working inside of peoples' mouths all day unappealing. This limits supply. Finally, a license is required to become a dentist. This also limits supply. So you can make a lot of money being a dentist, but do you want to?

On average, one occupation will end up being no more desirable than any other. If you want a very high salary, you will have to pay for it through high education or other entry costs, undesirable work or working conditions, long hours and little vacation time, and/or exceptional skill requirements. If you want an easy-to-enter and fun job that allows you lots of free time, you will have to pay for it through low wages.

But you are not average. You have particular skills and particular desires. These skills and desires should determine your career path. If you have the skill, if high income is particularly important to you, and if you find dentistry fascinating rather than undesirable, then for you the benefits may exceed the entry and other costs of entering this profession.

So survey yourself. Ask yourself:

- What benefits from work are of most importance to me? (Money? Free time? Social recognition? Meaningful accomplishments? Enjoyment from work?)
- What work do I most enjoy (or least dislike)?
- What skills or experience do I have (or can I get) that many others do not have?
- Are these skills and experience highly valued or demanded by somebody?

Then let your answers guide your career path.

But beware. Remember that many people like the same kinds of work. For example, many people want to be singers, artists, actresses and actors, and athletes. Consequently, supply is high and average salaries are low. You should enter occupations such as these only if your desire and skill is high *relative to your competition.*

Finally, new technologies and the availability of inexpensive foreign labor will lower or eliminate demand for low-skilled workers in the United States. For example, the demand for farmers and ranchers, secretaries, stock clerks, typists, and telephone operators is falling and no doubt will continue to fall. Meanwhile, the benefits of higher education and high-level skills are rising and will no doubt continue to rise (see Lesson 1).

Hence, the benefits associated with your investments of time, effort, and financial resources toward the development of a professional career will very likely be even larger in the future than they appear to be now.

5.   Choosing Where to Live

The problem of choosing a place to live is similar to the problem of choosing a career. Do you like mild temperatures, sunshine, beautiful beaches, and wonderful recreational opportunities? So does everyone else. It is very expensive to live in San Diego, Honolulu, or Miami Beach in large part because so many people would like to live there. In particular, competition among renters and home buyers bids up housing costs. This fact will be true locally as well as nationally. For example, within the metropolitan area you select to live, do you want to live in an attractive, safe neighborhood that offers great schools and an easy commute to downtown where you (and everyone else) work? So does everyone else. Thus, you can decide to live in desirable places, but you will pay for your decision through higher costs of living.

Don't be fooled. A potential employer may offer you a high nominal salary to work in a nice place like San Francisco. Sounds good, but the *real* income, or the purchasing power of the offer, may be low. Since the cost of living in San Francisco is so high, what might seem like a great salary may actually be a low salary in real terms. It is the real value, not the nominal or face value of money that determines what goods and services you can purchase. Indeed, employers located in nice places can more easily attract workers and (all else being equal) need only offer relatively low real wages.

So, Utopia does not exist. Your choice as to where to live should be based on your particular preferences. Do you enjoy mild temperatures, sunshine, and beautiful beaches significantly more than most other people? Do you mind lower real wages, congestion, and smaller homes significantly less than most other people? If your answers are yes and yes, then you should consider living in a place like Miami Beach. Otherwise, keep looking. Of course, the location of family and friends and your preference to be near (or far away from) them will also influence your decision about where to live.

Finally, your choice of career and your choice of where to live are joint decisions. Keep in mind that some careers limit mobility much more than others.

6.   Buying a Car

As with any purchase decision, when deciding whether to buy a car, you should think about and compare the additional benefits and the additional costs associated with the purchase. This general principle applies both to the purchase of a car and to decisions about buying particular features of a new car. It should be remembered, however, that the benefits (and maintenance costs) of a car occur over time while the purchase cost occurs up front. Thus, as when comparing the benefits and costs of attending college (see Lesson 1), the benefits and costs of buying a car must be *discounted* into *present value* terms before they can be directly compared.

In addition to general advice about how to think about and compare the benefits and costs of buying a car, economics also provides some very specific recommendations about how to get a good deal when buying a car. Auto sticker prices are usually starting points for negotiations. According to Edmonds.com, the average sticker price for a new car or light truck was roughly 15% higher than the average actual sales price. Why do car dealers make buyers haggle with them over price? Because they can make more profit by *price discriminating*—charging a higher price to some people and a lower price to others. By collecting information from and about you and by seeing how much time you are willing spend haggling, they can estimate what price you would be willing and able to pay. You may *signal* an *elastic demand* (a willingness to shop elsewhere if you don't get a low price) for buying a car if you convince the seller you are in no hurry, you are an informed buyer, you are not in total love with the seller's car, and that price is very important to you. If the seller suspects you have an *elastic de-*

mand, she may believe that lowering price may be the only way to make the sale. Instead, you may signal an *inelastic demand* for buying a car if you act impatiently, appear uninformed, express absolute love for the vehicle, and look, act, or provide information that indicates you are wealthy. If the seller suspects you have an inelastic demand, she may not lower the price and may instead try to sell you expensive features or a more expensive model. By charging high prices to buyers who care relatively less about price, and lower prices to buyers who care relatively more about price, dealers can make more sales and more profits.

The lessons to you are to look and act patient, informed (know the dealer cost!), not overly excited about buying a car, and relatively poor. You will likely get a lower price.

Economics provides additional tips for buying used cars. The *market* for used cars is plagued by the problem of *asymmetric information*. Car sellers have more information about the quality of their product than do car buyers. Suppose buyers believe that 50% of all used cars are "lemons" and 50% are good cars. Suppose buyers would pay $3,000 for a lemon and $7,000 for a good car, but that they can't tell whether a used car is a lemon until after they buy it. In this case, buyers would be willing to offer $5,000 (the average value they would receive) for a used car. But sellers know whether their cars are lemons or not. Thus, only owners of lemons would be willing to sell their cars for $5,000.

The lesson to you is to not buy a used car unless: (1) you know the owner is selling for a reason that is not related to the quality of the car (for example, they were transferred out of the country), (2) you are or decide to hire a good mechanic and thoroughly inspect the car (costly and still risky), or (3) the seller offers a warranty. Offering a warranty is the seller's way to signal that they are selling a good car (as well as a way to make a little extra profit if they sell the warranty). So ask the seller if they will provide or sell you a warranty. If they say yes, buy the car, but do not buy a warranty. You already know you are buying a reliable car.

7.   Buying or Selling a House

The decision to buy or sell a house involves many factors. At most bookstores you can find a variety of useful books that offer many tips about how and whether to buy or sell real estate. This lesson does not attempt to repeat such advice. Instead, it provides a few tips from economics that other books typically overlook.

Like all decisions, the decision to buy a house should be made by comparing benefits and costs. A full listing of all of the benefits and costs of buying versus renting is beyond the scope of this lesson. But one cost of buying worth noting here, because it is often overlooked, is the *opportunity cost* associated with making a down payment. Consider a very simplified example. Suppose the cost of renting a condo equals $1,000/month, but you also have the option to buy the condo. Suppose you could buy the condo for $120,000 with a 20% down payment ($24,000) and that owning the condo would reduce your total housing costs to $950/month. Which option is most cost effective? Assuming housing prices stay constant, you will get your $24,000 back after you sell your house. But this does not mean there is no cost associated with making the down payment. By using your savings for the down payment, you forego the opportunity to earn interest or other investment returns on these funds. If you could have earned 5% interest annually on the $24,000, you would forego $100/month [($24,000 × 0.05)/12 months] in interest. Thus, your full monthly costs of buying ($950 + $100) would exceed your monthly costs of renting. All else being equal, you should decide to rent.

When weighing the benefits and costs of a big decision such as buying a house, you should always remember that some things that count cannot be counted. For example, you may simply feel good about owning your own home. If so, then this real benefit should be factored into your decision, even if it can't be quantified.

The question of when to buy or sell a home depends in part on mortgage rates. Since most people have to borrow money to buy a house, low mortgage rates make monthly mortgage payments more affordable. However, when mortgage rates are low, home sellers can insist on higher prices. Thus, it is not necessarily a better time to buy your first house when mortgage rates are low. In fact, if you are sufficiently wealthy to buy a house without a mortgage, it would be better for you to buy during times when mortgage rates are high since home prices will be lower. From the seller's viewpoint, selling while mortgage rates are low makes good sense, especially if you are currently paying off a higher fixed-rate mortgage.

When obtaining a loan to buy a house, you must decide between fixed- or variable-rate mortgages. Many books on buying a house advise it is best to "lock in" mortgage rates when they are low by obtaining a long-term fixed-rate mortgage instead a variable-rate mortgage that may increase and increase your monthly payments in the future. But this advice may not be correct. First, it assumes that rates will not fall further. Mortgage rates are largely determined by *Federal Reserve* (Fed) policy and expectations about inflation. With some knowledge of macroeconomics and current events, you may be able to accurately predict the direction of mortgage rates. But so might banks. If banks believe interest rates will rise in the future, they may raise their long-term fixed rates well above their adjustable rates. That is, banks will factor their expectations regarding Fed policy and inflation into the mortgage rates they offer. So, unless you know something your bank doesn't about the future economy, it is not clear that fixed-rate mortgages will be a better deal than variable-rate mortgages, even when mortgage rates are currently low. Thus, you should rely more on other factors when choosing between fixed- and variable-rate mortgages, such as the length of time you expect to own the house (the shorter the stay, the more likely a variable rate is best) and your tolerance for uncertainty and risk (fixed rates provide more certainty).

Lastly, economic principles warn home sellers to be skeptical of some of the advice they may receive from real estate agents and brokers. For example, most people hire a real estate agent to sell their home for them. There are good reasons to do so. Besides showing your home and helping you deal with the paperwork and process, good agents bring in more potential buyers. More potential buyers increase your chances of receiving good offers. The opportunity to achieve a higher price and timelier sale may justify the significant cost of employing an agent. But it is important to recognize that your agent's interests are not entirely the same as yours. Agents are paid by commission based on a percentage of the sales price. Suppose you could offer your house for $200,000. If it sells, your listing agent may earn 3% of the sales price, or $6,000. Alternatively, suppose you offer your home for $220,000. In this case, you might expect your house to take several months longer to sell. When the house sold at this higher price, your agent would only make an additional $600, but you would make an additional $19,400. Thus, waiting may be well worth it to you, but not worth the extra months of work to your agent. Your agent has a stronger *incentive* to sell your house quickly than to sell your house at the highest possible price. Thus, agents may encourage you to offer and accept a lower price for your house than what would be in your best interest. Real estate agents understand their incentives; you should too. It is not surprising that Steven Levitt of the University of Chicago found that real estate agents leave their properties on the market longer and receive higher sales prices than do the home sellers whom they advise.

8.   Buying Insurance

Buying insurance is a gamble. For example, when you buy health insurance you are betting you will become ill. If you do not become ill, you lose from your decision to pay for the insurance. Of course, not buying insurance also is a gamble. The whole purpose of buying insurance is to reduce financial risk. Buying insurance reduces risk by accepting a certain but modest cost to avoid a small risk of a large cost. For most people, reducing risk is preferable. For example, most people would prefer to pay $200 every month to avoid a 1 in 100 chance each month of having to pay $20,000.

You should remember, however, that if you buy unsubsidized insurance, you generally will lose money. Insurance companies are in business to make money. Thus, on average, payoffs from insurance companies will be less than the insurance rates they charge.

With this fact in mind, consider the following recommendations. First, if you are relatively wealthy, do not insure yourself against relatively small losses. In the event of bad luck, you have enough wealth to insure yourself. For example, you may be better off dropping collision insurance on your car if replacing your car would not entail great hardship. Since average drivers will pay their insurance company more than they will get back in insurance claims, if you can insure yourself, you will most likely win in the long run. On the other hand, if you are wealthy, make sure to insure yourself against catastrophic losses. You can afford regular insurance payments easily, and you risk losing your wealth if you are not insured.

The opposite recommendations may be more appropriate if you are relatively poor. You may need to insure yourself against relatively small losses since even small losses might put you in financial jeopardy. On the other hand, if you have little or no wealth, you might consider skipping catastrophic coverage. You may have difficulty affording the premiums, and you do not have much wealth to lose in the event of a catastrophe.

Besides the obvious desire on the part of insurance companies to make profit, there are two problems with insurance markets that tend to keep insurance premiums high. The insurance market provides an example of *asymmetric information*. Buyers have more information than do sellers about the likelihood they will make insurance claims. This leads to the problem of *adverse selection*. Adverse selection occurs, for example, when individuals who know they are in poor health buy a disproportional amount of health insurance. Insurance companies know this. Unless they can get around this problem (see below), they will assume there is a relatively high probability that people who buy their insurance will file claims. Moreover, insurance companies know that once they provide insurance to people, they reduce the *incentives* for people to avoid risky behavior. This is called the *moral hazard* problem. For example, if you have fire insurance, you have less incentive to have and maintain smoke alarms. The adverse selection and moral hazard problems may require insurance companies to keep their premiums high to remain profitable.

All of this means the cost of insurance may be much higher than the expected payoffs to the average consumer. But you can use what you know about your particular risks to help you decide how much insurance to buy. If you believe your chances of making a claim are no higher than the average person's chances, your cost of buying insurance will no doubt be far greater than the expected payoffs from your insurance company. This does not necessarily mean you should decline to buy insurance, but it should at least make you think twice. On the other hand, if you have a much greater than average probability to making an insurance claim, and if your insurance company does not learn this fact, buying insurance may both reduce your risk and have a positive expected payoff.

Finally, some forms of insurance, such as life and health insurance, are often heavily subsidized by employers. Employer provided insurance also may be provided at a discount by insurance companies. By negotiating a deal with your employer to provide insurance to all or most employees, an insurer may avoid the adverse selection problem. When employers cover part of the cost and insurers offer discounts, buying insurance through your employer is often a very good deal.

9.   Borrowing and Using a Credit Card

Given the high rate of return to investments in education today, it usually makes more sense for college students to be borrowers than to be savers. Generally, college students should delay attempts to save for their future until they have entered the workforce and paid back their educational loans. It makes little sense to put a significant amount of money into a relatively low-interest savings account or certificate of deposit if you are still paying off college or other loans at a higher interest rate.

But is it wise for college students to go heavy into debt to finance their education? Perhaps it is. If the costs of borrowing are less than the expected benefits from the investment, then it makes sense to go into debt. Since the returns to higher education are so high in the United States, it may be worth going into significant debt if that is what it takes to graduate. Of course it may make most sense to attend your community college and/or state college instead of a private college so that you (or your family) will not incur nearly as much debt. But this is a different matter. The point here is that it can be wise to owe money.

One form of borrowing, however, that everyone should be particularly careful about is borrowing through the use of credit cards. There are many good reasons to use a credit card: (1) you can easily purchase products over the phone or internet and you are protected if the goods do not arrive, (2) you get a record of your transactions, (3) you don't have to carry around as much cash which could be lost or stolen (if your credit card is stolen, the most you are supposed to be liable for is $50), and (4) you get to use someone else's money for a while. Credit cards are not money. When you use a credit card, you are borrowing money. You pay the loan off with money each month when you write your check to your credit card company. As long as you pay your full balance on time, you don't have to pay interest. When you pay by credit card instead of cash, you may continue earning interest on your money. If you are going to make a large purchase, you could time it to maximize your interest by buying the item just after the date of your billing cycle.

But all of the benefits of using credit cards are outweighed by the costs if credit cards are not used wisely. If you do not pay off your balance by the due date, you will have to pay interest on your balance. Credit card interest rates are very high relative to other interest rates in the economy. Credit card loans entail a relatively high risk of default, and this risk premium is in part passed on to card holders in the form of high interest rates. Consequently, short of emergency, you should discipline yourself to not run a balance on your card. If you are running a balance, your best investment will almost always be to pay off your credit card bill.

Unfortunately, many people do run credit card debts. Psychological factors may contribute to this problem. Studies indicate that people tend to spend more when they are using plastic than when they buy things using cash. Why people seem to spend more with credit cards is unclear. What is clear is that running high credit card debts is a very serious problem for many young adults today.

10.   Saving and Investing

Once your income exceeds your basic needs and your high interest loans are paid off, it may be time for you to start saving for your future. Recent macroeconomic events suggest you may have extra reason to save. During the early 2000s, tax cuts, plus increased military and other federal spending helped cause high budget deficits in the United States. As a result, your taxes may need to be higher in the future to service the rising federal debt. More worrisome, your taxes may need to be raised in the future to cope with the forthcoming Social Security and Medicare budget shortfall (see Lesson 96). Moreover, if taxes are raised to deal with these problems, this could trigger an economic slowdown, or *recession*. All else being equal, people will have less money to spend, businesses will sell less goods and services, and fewer workers will be hired. Thus, your risk of unemployment may rise, giving you even more reason to save. Finally, terrorism imposes risk to the macroeconomy and to your financial security. While this paragraph may paint an overly gloomy picture of our economic future (technological progress, for example, will tend to raise standards of living in the future), it serves to alert you to the risks of not saving for a rainy day.

To explore specific options and strategies for investing your money, you may want to consult a book on personal finance. Economics does not focus on specific investment strategies, but it does provide general advice about saving and investing your money.

Saving inevitably involves a trade-off between risk and *liquidity* on one hand and return on the other. High-risk investments (such as the purchase of an individual high-tech company's stock) can be expected to yield greater returns *on average* than low-risk investments (such as a U.S. savings bond). Security is not free. You pay for relatively certain returns by accepting lower average returns. The degree of risk you should accept depends on your financial status and personal preference. In any case, you may be able to reduce your investment risks through diversification strategies. Holding wealth in a wide variety of assets (such as money, certificates of deposit, bonds, stocks, real estate, etc.) reduces overall risk.

Less liquid investments that tie up your money tend to yield higher returns than do more liquid investments. For example, a 5-year certificate of deposit will yield greater interest than a more liquid 3-month certificate of deposit. You pay for greater liquidity by accepting lower returns. The amount of liquidity you should forego depends on the likelihood you will need to convert your investment into cash in the near future. Do not keep your money in a low-interest checking, money market, or savings account if you are saving the money for retirement many years from now.

Finally, it is important for savers to understand the difference between *nominal* and *real* interest rates. Nominal interest rates are the rates banks advertise. Real interest rates are nominal interest rates adjusted for *inflation*. The real interest rate of your savings in a bank reflects the increase in purchasing power you earn from your loan. Since you are concerned with the purchasing power of your money, the real interest rate is important to you. For example, if you purchase a certificate of deposit at a 3% (nominal) interest rate, and if the inflation rate is 4%, your investment will lose purchasing power! (This story becomes sadder if we factor in the taxes you may need to pay on your 3% interest.)

On the other hand, the nominal interest rate is most important to your decision regarding how much of your assets you should hold in the form of money. Money is the most liquid asset. You need to hold money (cash and checking accounts) to facilitate everyday financial transactions. (You can't buy a Big Mac with a share of stock!) But there is a cost or *opportunity cost* of holding money. When you hold money, you forego the opportunity to gain interest or other returns from investing the money. When nominal interest rates (reflecting high real interest rates and/or high inflation) are high, the cost of holding money is high. During such times you should keep your wallets, purses, and no-interest checking accounts thin.

11. Playing the Stock Market

One way corporations raise money is by selling stock. A stock is a claim to partial ownership of the profits a firm makes. Millions of people buy stocks as a financial investment. Stockholders make money by collecting dividends (when corporations distribute dividends to stockholders out of profits) or by earning capital gains (when stockholders sell stock after stock prices appreciate). However, stock values can, and sometimes do, fall substantially. Thus, investing in stocks involves significant risk.

While paying off credit cards and investing in your own education are higher priorities for most young adults, at some point you probably should buy stocks as a long-term investment. Historically, average returns in the stock market are relatively high. But which stocks should you buy?

You can get an earful of advice from stock "analysts" and brokers. But you need not waste your time and money employing these so-called "experts." (Did you ever wonder why these folks do not simply take their own advice, buy low and sell high, get rich, and give up their 9 to 5 jobs?) A surprising economic theory strongly advises that you can pick stocks every bit as successfully as the "experts." In fact, so could a blind ape throwing darts at the financial page!

Like all prices in our economy, stock prices are determined by the market forces of *supply* and *demand*. If expected profitability rises, demand for stocks will rise, driving stock prices upward. An important feature of the stock market is that it is an extremely *efficient market*—it incorporates all new information that could affect a stock's price virtually instantaneously. So, if a company publicly announces it expects to make greater than previously expected profits, the company's stock price will rise instantly after the announcement. You will not be able to benefit from this announcement because before you can say "buy," the stock's price will have already risen. It turns out that the only way to "beat the market" is to know something about the direction of stock prices that no one else knows. But such information would be insider information, which is illegal to act upon. While a full explanation of the theory of stock prices is beyond the scope of this book, the bottom line for you is that neither you nor your stockbroker can pick winning stocks any better than anyone else. Economists have tested the efficient market theory of stock prices over and over again and found the same result—in the absence of insider information, picking individual stocks is essentially a random exercise.

While neither economists nor anyone else can tell you what stocks will appreciate in the future, economics can give you some important advice about investing in stocks:

(1)   Buy: As a long-term investment, the stock market is probably a good bet;

(2)   Guess: Do not pay for stock picking advice. You can do just as well guessing;

(3)   Hold: Since stock picking is a guessing game, don't trade. Trading involves fees that will eat into your investment returns; and

(4)   Diversify: Do not put all your eggs in one basket. Own a diversified stock portfolio, such as a mutual fund. This is an effective way to minimize risk.

12. Marrying

Even marriages are determined in a market. The marriage market [as well as the market for dating and sex (except for prostitution)] is a market without money. Rather, marriages are formed via *barter*. Each person finds someone they want who simultaneously wants them. Then each person can trade their "services" to their partner. Unfortunately, markets without money involve high search and other transactions costs and are thus highly inefficient. As a result, it typically takes much time, effort, and expense for people to find acceptable partners, and many people remain lonely.

Formal engagement and marriage are ways to limit competition in the barter market for partners. For example, why do men often give their future spouse an engagement ring? There are at least three plausible reasons: (1) they get happiness from making their partner happy (and they believe giving an engagement ring is the best thing they could buy their partner to make them happy), (2) they think by giving the ring they will be more liked and desired (i.e., the gift will increase the *demand* for their services), and/or (3) they believe the ring when worn will warn off potential competition. Marriage itself is a way to limit competition. It imposes potentially high legal and/or societal costs on partners who stray and competitors who compete. The bottom line is that while love and altruism play important roles in most romantic relationships, self-interest typically plays a large role too. After all, if everyone were concerned only about their partner's happiness, why would anyone wish to limit their partner's "opportunities"?

In addition to limiting competition, providing a certain degree of security, and the obvious benefits from close companionship, marriage provides various other benefits. Here the focus is on less understood economic benefits, rather than emotional or societal benefits that might result from marriage. For example, living together in marriage can be a more efficient living arrangement than living alone. Living with someone permits gains from specialization. Each individual can perform those tasks for which they have *comparative advantage* in performing. You may dislike shopping and always forget to buy something, while your partner may dislike cleaning and never clean thoroughly. By living together, you could do all the cleaning and your partner could do all the shopping and you may both be better off. You could instead pay someone to do all of the various household tasks you do not want to do, but this would incur high *transaction costs*, such as the costs of finding and negotiating with someone to do the tasks. Forming a marriage, like forming a business, serves to reduce the everyday transactions costs associated with getting work internal to the organization (or household) done. Finally, living together allows people to share *non-rival goods*. For example, consider a backyard swimming pool. If you use the pool, it does not take away from your partner's use of the pool. So, both you and your partner could use the pool at the cost of one pool.

Of course, the efficiencies associated with living together may be acquired whether you legally marry your partner or not. Moreover, even greater efficiencies may be achievable if more than two people move in together, specialize in performing tasks, reduce transactions costs, and share non-rival goods.

Marriage also imposes certain costs. There are various obvious costs of marriage, such as potentially sizeable wedding costs for those who choose to have a wedding. There are also less obvious costs. For some people, one cost that may not be anticipated is higher taxes. The U.S. federal income tax is a *progressive tax*, meaning that it disproportionately taxes people who earn higher incomes. For example, if you make $30,000 per year your *marginal* tax rate (the percent of the next dollar you make you must pay in federal taxes) will be lower than if you make $100,000 per year. The so-called "marriage penalty" occurs when two-income partners marry and their incomes get added together for tax purposes. While the married marginal tax rate is lower than the single marginal tax rate all else being equal, when both spouses' incomes are combined, the resulting marginal tax rate is often higher, especially if both spouses make similar incomes. In this case, you may be better off taxwise living together without being married (though Congress is moving toward reducing this marriage penalty). On the other hand, if your partner doesn't work, you will save taxes by marrying.

Another less obvious cost of marriage involves lost "opportunities." By being married (assuming you remain faithful), you forego the opportunity to be involved with other partners. This cost is different for different people. If you are considered particularly attractive and personable, you will forego more opportunities by being married than most other people. Your *opportunity cost* of being married would be particularly high. Thus, you should be more reluctant than most other people to marry (and more likely to divorce if you do marry). This advice is especially relevant for famous people (see Lesson 57).

Are the benefits of marriage worth the costs? Results from a study by economists David Blanchflower from Dartmouth University and Andrew Oswald from the University of Warwick suggest that the net benefits of a lasting marriage may be quite large. They found that on average, individuals in lasting marriages report being equally as happy as individuals who are divorced but who make $100,000 more income per year. One might infer from this result that a lasting marriage is worth something like $100,000/year to the average married person. However, another interpretation of this result is that the cost of being divorced is $100,000/year (a cost you may never have to pay if you never get married). In any case, the lesson to be learned from this study is to take enormous care when selecting a marriage partner since much of your happiness will likely rest on the durability of your marriage.

To summarize, as with other big decisions you must make throughout your life, the decision to marry should involve a consideration and comparison of benefits and costs. This fact remains true even if the major source of your benefits from marriage is the happiness of your partner.

13. Raising Kids

The decision to have and raise children entails major economic costs. Not only must parents incur the costs associated with feeding, clothing, sheltering, educating, entertaining, etc., their children, they must also incur substantial *opportunity costs* associated with the time spent caring for their children. For example, a major component of the cost to families of raising children is the income that cannot be earned when one spouse must stay home to care for his or her children. With the rise in opportunities for women in the workplace throughout the last several decades, the opportunity cost of raising children has increased significantly in the United States. This may explain why American woman are having fewer children today than in the past (see Lesson 58). Still, as any parent knows, the benefits from having and raising children also can be very great, though few of these benefits are easily quantifiable.

Once you have children, lessons from economics can help you raise them. Obviously, raising children is not an entirely economic matter. Many books on parenting exist to assist you with this daunting task. The focus here is on lessons from economics that can help you raise happier and more socially well-behaved children. In particular, two lessons from economics should be kept in mind by all parents: (1) *incentives* drive behavior, and (2) free choice is generally beneficial.

Like adults, children respond to both positive and negative incentives. Parents partly control the incentives facing their children. A key for parents is to be aware of the incentives their actions or inaction impose on their children. For example, if you give your son a cookie (a positive incentive) to get him to stop crying, he may stop crying. But you may also create a longer-run incentive for him to cry more frequently (whenever he wants a cookie). Or, does your son interrupt you when you are talking with others? Do you stop talking and speak to your son when they do? If so, then your son will learn that the benefits of interrupting exceed the nonexistent costs and he will continue the behavior.

You may choose to use financial incentives to induce your children to consider the full costs of their actions and behave in a more socially beneficial manner. For example, if your daughter has savings that she has earned or accumulated through allowances, you may wish to make her pay for her costly behavior. Does your daughter always forget to turn off lights, appliances, or the TV when she leaves the house? Why should she remember? You pay the bills. Make her pay for the electricity she wastes and the problem will be resolved. Or, can't get your son to clean his room? Routinely make him pay (either the value of your time or the price to pay a maid) to have the room cleaned every few months if he doesn't do it himself. Your problem will be solved whether your son cleans his room or not.

Some people object to the idea of offering or imposing financial incentives for children. Nevertheless, some kind of incentive has to be imposed to induce children to do tasks they don't want to do. Routinely imposed financial incentives may avoid needless animosity and other emotional side effects of other forms of punishment such as yelling, threatening, and spanking. Moreover, if children are made to pay the costs of their behavior, they will learn there are logical consequences of their actions, but they will still be granted choices. If they really hate one of their chores, they could choose to pay (if they have earned enough savings) for someone else to do it. Children would be happier having this option, and they could be left feeling responsible and guilt-free when they choose to exercise it.

Children often know what is best for them. When they do, parents should let children make their own decisions. For example, when the famous prize-winning economist Milton Friedman took his young children on overnight train trips, he asked them whether they wanted sleeping berths or would they rather sit up and keep the money the berths would have cost (they always took the money). Except when a parent judges that their child's decision may do irreversible or serious harm to themselves or to someone else, letting their child choose for themselves will either make the child happier or it will teach the child a valuable lesson.

14. Asking for and Getting a Raise

Asking for a raise should be viewed as a negotiation. Negotiations are economic events because the outcome of negotiations depends very much on perceived benefits, costs, and incentives.

As a negotiator, you would like to do whatever you can to increase the perceived benefit (or decrease the perceived cost) to the person or group you are negotiating with of agreeing to your position. When negotiating a raise, you will want to convince your employer that the benefits he or she will receive from granting the raise will exceed the costs. But what actions can you take to influence your employer's benefit-cost calculation?

First, you must attempt to understand the nature and extent of the perceived costs to your employer of not giving you a raise. The perceived cost to your employer of not giving you a raise will depend on the consequences your employer perceives of not giving you a raise. If, for example, your employer believes there will be no repercussions of denying your raise (because she or he believes you will continue working at your job at the same level of productivity), your employer will have little *incentive* to grant you the raise. On the other hand, if your employer believes you will quit your job if you don't get a raise, then the perceived cost to your employer would equal the profits your employer would lose if you quit. Thus, you can increase the perceived cost of being denied a raise, and the likelihood you will get the raise, by convincing your employer that you will quit if you don't get the raise.

You can simply tell your employer that you will leave your job if you don't get the raise, but your employer may not believe you. You may need to develop a credible threat. For example, if you could obtain a good job offer from another employer and share this offer with your current employer, you would be in a much stronger negotiating position (even if you have no intention of ever accepting the other employer's offer). Unfortunately, it may not be easy for you to obtain a good job offer from another employer. Another somewhat aggressive strategy to create a credible threat would be to tell all of your co-workers that you will quit if you don't get a raise. This might impose a "humiliation cost" on yourself of staying in your job if you don't get the raise. Your employer, knowing that you would be humiliated if you stayed in your job if denied the raise, may be convinced that you will quit and, thus, be more likely to grant your raise.

Given that your employer believes you may quit if you don't get a raise, you can influence the employer's cost of not granting the raise by increasing your perceived productivity. Profit maximizing employers will pay an employee no more than the extra revenue (or *marginal revenue product*) the employee generates for the business. The more productive your employer believes you are, the higher the perceived cost of not giving you the raise and possibly losing your services. But productivity is often hard to measure. Employers may rely on "*signals*" from employees to estimate their productivity. One commonly used signal is hours worked. You may be able to increase your chances of obtaining a raise by working late, even if you do not increase your productivity. Indeed, many working professionals work well beyond their paid 40 hours per week to send signals to their management.

Finally, managers who hire and promote employees do not always make their decisions based strictly on the profit maximization criterion. In larger organizations, it is often difficult for owners (especially stockholders) to monitor the every day decisions made by managers. Managers (the agents) may at times pursue their own interests instead of the profit-maximizing interests of the business's owner (the principal) without penalty. This creates the so-called *principal-agent problem*. When managers pursue their own interests when making hiring and promotion decisions, they may use criteria unrelated to profit maximization such as their personal preferences regarding who they would prefer to supervise and promote. Thus, by expressing how important a raise is to you and by signaling that you will be grateful and pleasant to be around if you get the raise (and disgruntled and unpleasant to supervise

if you don't), you may influence the manager's personal benefit-cost calculus in favor of granting your raise.

15.   Trying

Many of us have been offered the advice "Try your best at
whatever you do." But trying your best at something is usually
bad economics. Trying your best at an activity involves dedi-
cating all of your time and energy to the activity. But at some
point your time and effort will experience *diminishing returns*
and high *opportunity costs*. For example, if you decide to "try
your best" to be a professional athlete and practice day and
night, the last hour of practice would not improve your game
significantly (it may make it worse due to fatigue) and would
entail significant opportunity costs (such as the chance to eat or
rest). Thus, at some point, the costs of practicing more hours
will likely exceed the benefits from the additional practice.
Economics argues that you should try hard to achieve goals
that are important to you. But it also argues that you shouldn't
try your hardest when the costs of doing so exceed the benefits.
Tradeoffs are inevitable. This fact applies to your decisions
about spending your time and energy, as well as to your decisions about spending your money.

You also may have been offered the advice "If you don't
succeed at first, try, try again." While it never makes sense to
try to do something that is not worth doing, sometimes this advice is good economics.

Consider the following example. Suppose you wish to sell your
old car. The car is worthless to you, but you expect it will sell
for $1,000 if you aggressively advertise. You spend $500 on
advertisements in a local newspaper (The Washington Times).
The car does not sell.

One day you tell your sad story to your friend. He says to
you, "I know why your car didn't sell. You advertised in the
wrong newspaper. If you run the same number of ads in the
Washington Post, I guarantee it will sell. In fact, if it doesn't
sell, I'll buy it from you for $1,000!" You say to your friend,
"Great, thanks for the advice. By the way, what will it cost me

to run the same number of ads in the Post?" He answers, "$800." Should you advertise your car again?

When I ask this question to my new economics students, the vast majority instinctively respond—"No way!" But good economics requires that you advertise again. The fact that your first attempt to sell your car failed should have no relevance to your decision about whether to try again. The $500 you spent advertising in the Times is a *sunk cost*; it is gone no matter what you do. Relevant now are the relative benefits and costs associated with your next decision. Advertising in the Post will yield a guaranteed $1,000, and it would cost you $800. This is a good deal. In the end you will be out $300 from the whole car sale exercise, but this is better than being out $500 if you don't advertise in the Post. In this case, you definitely should try again.

16. Spending Your "Free" Time

Time is scarce and valuable. How you use your time depends on your personal preferences and the options available to you. However, economics provides a logical framework you can use to think clearly and systematically about allocating your time.

Suppose it is Saturday afternoon and you must decide how to spend your time. You believe your best options are to (1) play tennis, (2) go to work to make $10/hour, or (3) study economics. How should you decide what to do?

First, you should recognize that using your time is not cost-less. Just because you own your time does not mean it is free for you to use it. The *opportunity cost* of spending time studying economics, for example, is the value you forego by not spending your time doing your next best alternative—either playing tennis or working, whichever yields the highest benefits to you.

Second, you should *think marginally*. You should ask yourself the question, "What are the additional or marginal benefits I would get from spending another hour doing each of these activities?" So if between 12 and 1 P.M., it was worth $20 to you (in terms of what you would learn and your improved chance to earn a higher grade) to study economics, $15 to play tennis (in terms of fun), and $10 to work, you should spend this hour studying (your marginal benefit equals $20, and your marginal cost equals $15, since $15 is the value of the next best alternative you are foregoing).

Lastly, you should keep in mind the principle of *diminishing returns*. Just because it makes most sense for you to study between 12 and 1 P.M. does not mean you should study all afternoon. At some point, the rate of increase in learning from studying will decrease. Once you have read your book and notes three times, reading them again wouldn't provide much additional learning. Plus, at some point, you may become sleepy or mentally tired which could slow your rate of learning. So perhaps studying between 1 P.M. and 2 P.M. only produces $8 of value to you. In this case, you should stop studying at 1 P.M. and play tennis for an hour. But of course, after a while, you will get tired or bored playing tennis. You might then choose to go to work for the rest of the day.

But should you really think carefully about all of these principles and try to quantify the marginal benefits of each activity every time you must decide how to spend your time? Of course not—it would be bad economics to do so. It does not make sense to spend too much time thinking about how to best spend your time. But when you are faced with important time management decisions, investing some thought using this logical framework may be worth it to you.

Finally you should recognize the highly fictitious nature of the example we just studied. After all, the value of studying economics all afternoon surely exceeds any opportunity cost.

CHAPTER 2:
Make Better Business Decisions

Introduction

Basic principles of economics, such as the 3-step approach to making decisions outlined in the Introduction to Part One, can and should be applied when making business-related decisions. If you wish to maximize the profitability of your business, you will want to learn how to apply these principles.

As when applied to personal decision making, economic principles alone will rarely provide definitive solutions to business problems that will apply in all circumstances. Rather, economics teaches a logical approach to business decision making and provides numerous tips that can be used to help you maximize the success of your business. So let's start using economics to help make some of the most fundamental and important business decisions every business will encounter.

17. Should You Start a Business?

It will always make sense for you to start a business if your business can make *economic profit*. Economic profit, however, is not the same thing as accounting profit (total revenues – total expenses). Economic profit takes into account all *opportunity costs* associated with starting a business.

For example, suppose you own a building and you are deciding whether to open and manage a small grocery store business in your building. Your reliable accountant estimates that to operate your store you will need to spend $5,000 for supplies, $3,000 in wages for part-time workers, and $1,000 for utilities each month. Your accountant also estimates your sales revenue would equal $10,000/month. She thus recommends you open the store because it would be profitable ($1,000/month). Is she right?

From the viewpoint of an accountant, she is correct. You may, for example, have to pay taxes on this $1,000 "profit."

35

But your grocery store would almost surely not make a positive economic profit. To compute economic profit you must include all costs associated with opening and running your business, not just your explicit expenditures ($9,000). For example, you must include the opportunity cost associated with spending your time managing the store. If instead of managing the store you could have been driving a taxi and making $2,000/month, this $2,000 would be another cost of operating the store. You must also include the opportunity cost associated with using your building in this business. Just because you own the building doesn't mean it is free to use it! By employing the building as a grocery store, you would forego the opportunity to rent it out or use it for some other purpose. If instead of using the building as a store you could rent the building for $1,000/month, then this $1,000 would be another cost of operating the store. Thus, in this example, economic profit is negative ($10,000 − $9,000 − $2,000 − $1,000 = −$2,000) and you should not open the store. You would be better off driving a taxi and renting out your building. The test for opening a business should be positive economic profit, not positive accounting profit.

To start a business, you would most likely need to invest some of your own money in the business or borrow money from a bank or from investors. Whether using your own money or borrowed money, another important cost associated with starting a business is the opportunity cost associated with interest payments. Suppose, for example, you can borrow money at a 5% interest rate to start your business. You should do so only if the borrowed money is expected to earn a rate of return of at least 5% in your business. Suppose instead you use your own funds to start your business. The cost of using your own funds is implicit, but there is still a cost. If your savings are earning 5% interest in a bank, then you would forego this 5% return by withdrawing the money and using it in your business. Again, you should do so only if the money is expected to earn a rate of return of at least 5% in your business.

Many businesses take time before they become profitable. Suppose you expect your business to be unprofitable initially and then profitable afterward. How can you decide whether to start the business? To compare initial losses with future profits, you must first put all loss and profit estimates into *present value* terms by *discounting* future profits and losses. For example, suppose you expect your business to lose $100,000 during its first year and earn $52,000 (adjusted for inflation) dollars the next two years. Would this be a profitable business after three years? The answer depends on the prevailing interest rate. A $1 profit next year does not equate with a $1 loss this year, because the lost initial year dollar could have earned you interest by next year [for example, if the interest rate is 5%, by next year your loss would equal $(1 + 0.05)]. Thus, your future profits must be discounted before comparing them to your initial losses. [Assuming an interest rate of 5% and applying the formula for discounting found in many textbooks, the present value of your future profits in the example above would equal $52,000/(1 + 0.05) + $52,000/(1 + 0.05)^2 = $96,690 < $100,000$. Thus, you should not start this business unless you expected to earn additional profits after year three.]

Finally, there are other factors you will need to consider to fully count and properly compare the benefits and costs of starting a business. For example, you should consider the risk associated with starting a new business. The future demand for your products is uncertain and will depend on various factors such as consumer tastes, the availability of substitute products from competitors, and macroeconomic conditions. The future costs of producing your products also will be uncertain since input costs can be volatile and technology advances at unpredictable speed. Thus, when deciding whether to open a business you should consider and factor in your personal tolerance for risk. You should compare your expected revenues over time with your expected costs over time, but you may wish to include a risk premium within your expected cost estimate.

18.   What Product Should You Sell?

The simple answer to the question of what products or services to sell is that you should sell a product as long as you expect to make *economic profit* from selling it. But, of course, estimating profitability is a complex real world exercise. The objective of this lesson is to identify a few key factors you should consider when assessing the likelihood that a particular product or service will be profitable to produce and sell.

Obviously, when deciding whether to begin selling a particular good you will need to estimate the *demand* for the good. You will want to sell what consumers want to buy at a price sufficiently high to outweigh your production and sales costs.

But another critical factor to consider when deciding whether to begin selling a good is the nature of the competition you will face. Does or could other businesses sell the same good at the same cost (such as in a *perfectly competitive* market)? Even if you are the first business to offer a good, you would not be able to make long-run economic profits if other businesses eventually sell the very same product at the same cost of production. Any profits you may make in the short run would attract competitors into your market, increasing the *supply* of the product, and driving price downward until no one could make above zero economic profit. Only if you have a unique ability that allows you to produce the product or service at less cost than your competitors could you maintain profits selling the product or service. Thus, two important factors you should consider when deciding what to sell are: (1) the likelihood of direct competition, and (2) your ability to produce the product at a lower cost than your competitors.

Avoiding competition is difficult, but not impossible. If you sell a product that is a little different than any competitor's product (such as in a *monopolistically competitive* market) you may obtain some degree of *monopoly* power allowing you to keep price higher and make profits. But here, too, competitors selling similar products may enter your market and advertise their product to compete for your customers. Demand for your product may fall and you may be forced to advertise which will drive up your costs. The long run result will be zero economic profits.

But it may be possible, especially with the government's help, to block competition. For example, if you are able to develop a unique product, you may be able to obtain a copyright or patent on the product. With a copyright or patent, you are granted the exclusive legal right to sell your product for a number of years. During these years, you could sell your product as a monopolist. You could keep your price high without fear of competition and sustain above zero economic profits. It is possible to produce and sell a product that maintains monopoly status and profits without legal protection (Microsoft's windows operating system is a probable example). But it is very difficult to do so. The marketplace is vibrant. Profits attract competitors like honey attracts bees.

Another consideration when deciding whether to begin producing and selling a product involves the nature of the costs associated with producing the product. The production of some products experience *economies of scale*. Economies of scale occur when producing more of a product drives down the *average cost* of producing the product. This happens when certain inputs in a production process can be used more efficiently if used on a greater scale. For example, by increasing the scale of production businesses can sometimes reduce per unit costs through specialization of their workforce and through more efficient use of their machines and equipment.

To illustrate the economies of scale concept and how this concept relates to your decision about what products to sell, consider the following simplified example. Suppose you are opening a small neighborhood deli and you are trying to decide whether to sell only sandwiches or to also sell pizza. To sell a pizza, you will have to buy a pizza oven each year for $1,000 and it will cost you $3 per pizza made in materials and other costs. Since you must buy an oven to make one pizza or to make 1,000 pizzas, your cost per pizza will be much lower if you produce many pizzas. For example, if you make 1,000 pizzas your average cost to produce a pizza would equal

$1,000/1,000 pizzas + $3,000/1,000 pizzas = $4/pizza. But if you only produced 100 pizzas with your oven your average cost would equal $1,000/100 pizzas + $300/1,000 pizzas = $10.30/pizza. At an average cost of $10.30 you would no doubt find it difficult to compete with the larger scale Pizza Huts and Dominos Pizza operations in your neighborhood. Thus, you should not produce and sell pizza or any other good that experiences significant economies of scale unless you believe you will be able to sell enough of them.

19.   How Much of Your Product Should You Sell?

The general rule when deciding how much to do of any activity is to continue doing the activity as long as the additional (or *marginal*) benefits of the activity exceed the additional (or *marginal*) costs. When the additional benefits no longer exceed the additional costs, stop the activity. To apply this general rule to the question of how much of your product or service you should sell, you must estimate the additional benefits and additional costs of selling more of your product. A business is in business to make as much profit as possible. Profit equals total revenue – total costs. When you sell more of a good, you will accrue additional revenues and additional costs. Thus, as long as your additional revenues exceed your additional costs, you should continue producing and selling your product.

A closer study of the concepts of marginal revenue and marginal cost is instructive. When you sell one more of your good, by how much does your revenue increase? The answer depends on whether you drive down the price of your good when you sell more of the good. If the *market structure* you compete within approximates a *perfectly competitive* market where numerous businesses are selling the same good you are, your sales will be too small a percentage of the total market sales to affect the market price of your good. Thus, if you sell one more of your good, the marginal revenue you will receive will equal the price of the good. But if you sell your good in a less than fully competitive industry and own some degree of *monopoly* power over your good, the marginal revenue you will receive from selling one more of your good will be less than the price of the good, since by selling more you will drive down the price you receive on all of your sales of the good. In this case, the more you sell of your good, the lower the price and marginal revenue you receive.

Meanwhile, if you produce and sell more of your good, you will likely drive up your marginal costs of production. For example, suppose you are a farmer growing corn. To increase your corn production, you will need more inputs or *factors of production* such as land, machines, labor, fertilizer, irrigation water, etc. But in the near term, it may not be feasible to increase some of your inputs, such as your land and buildings. As you increase the use of a variable input (such water) holding other inputs (such as land) fixed, at some point *diminishing returns* will occur and it will become increasing difficult and costly to produce more of your good. Even if you can increase all of your inputs eventually, your marginal production costs may rise since you may drive up your costs of buying your inputs. For example, to produce more you may have to acquire more expensive land and employ overtime, higher wage, or less productive workers.

Thus, if you produce and sell more of your product or service your marginal revenue will remain constant or fall and your marginal costs will likely rise at some level of production. The quantity where marginal revenue equates with marginal cost is the quantity that will maximize your profits.

20. What Price Should You Charge?

Your decision about what price to charge for your product or service is linked to your decision about how much to sell of your product or service and will depend on the *market structure* of the industry within which you compete. There are at least three distinct scenarios.

First, suppose you sell your good within a *perfectly competitive* (or nearly perfectly competitive) market. In a perfectly competitive market, there are an infinite number of sellers all selling exactly the same good. In this case, you will not be able to charge a higher price for your good than the price your competitors charge. If you do, no one will buy from you since they can easily find someone else to buy the good from at the lower price. You also will not be able to charge a lower price than the price your competitors charge and still make profit. In such an industry, competition will drive the market price downward until no seller can make above zero *economic profit*. Charging a lower price than the price everyone else is charging will not allow you to cover your costs. Thus, if there are a great number of competitors selling the exact same good as you are selling, you (and every other seller) will be forced to charge the same price, like it or not.

Suppose instead that you sell your product or service within an *oligopoly*. An oligopoly is an industry market structure where only a few businesses compete with each other. Because of interdependence between businesses in an oligopoly, determining the price that will maximize profits for any business within oligopoly is tricky and involves strategy. For example, suppose American and three other airlines offer round-trip flights from Washington, D.C., to Raleigh for $200. If you were the president of American, would you lower this fare? Since all four airlines are selling essentially the same service, if you lower your price only a little you may be able to increase American's market share greatly. But what if the other airlines decide to match your price reduction? Worse, what if they reduce prices further than you do and a price war unfolds? In this case, all four airlines will be worse off. Instead, should you raise American's fare? Yes, if you believe your competitors will follow your lead, but you'll lose much of your market share if they don't. Hence, pricing within an oligopolistic market requires strategy and a careful consideration of your competitors' moves.

Finally, a third market structure scenario applies if no one else is selling the exact same product or service you are selling. In this case, you will own some degree of *monopoly* power. With monopoly control, you are a price maker rather than a price taker and your pricing options are less constrained. How do you decide what price will maximize your profits? From Lesson 19 you learned that to maximize profits you must sell the quantity of your good where *marginal revenue* no longer exceeds *marginal cost.* Therefore, to maximize your profits, you must charge the price that will result in this profit maximizing quantity being purchased. To know exactly what price this is, you will need to estimate the *demand* schedule or curve for your product or service. You may be able to use past sales records or employ market research techniques such as consumer surveys to collect and analyze price and quantity data to estimate the actual demand curve for your good.

In practice, however, it may be difficult for you to estimate the demand for your product or service. Short of estimating a full demand curve, you should be able to estimate the *elasticity of demand* for your good (your % change in sales if you change your price 1%) by considering the availability of *substitutes* for, and the relative expense of, your good. All else being equal, the fewer substitutes available and the smaller the relative cost of your good, the less *elastic* demand will be and the higher price you will be able to charge for your good without losing significant sales. Moreover, given an estimate of the elasticity of demand, you can use a practical "rule of thumb" for pricing that economists have developed to help managers set prices to maximize their profits. This rule of thumb states that the price markup over your marginal cost should equal the inverse of the elasticity of demand.

For example, suppose you sell Yummy Cola. You know there are substitutes for your product, but no other cola has the same yummy taste as your cola. You also know your cola is a relatively inexpensive good. Even without data, you should expect your cola (even more so than cola drinks in general) to have a high elasticity of demand (say 10, meaning that a 1% increase in price would lead to a 10% reduction in sales). Suppose your marginal cost is $0.90 per bottle. Then using the pricing rule of thumb, your profit maximizing mark up over price should be approximately 1/10 or 10%, and your profit maximizing price should be approximately $0.99 per bottle, or nine cents greater than your marginal cost.

The above advice assumes you can only charge one price for your product or service. But if you have monopoly power over your product, you may be able to increase your profits by employing *price discrimination*. Price discrimination involves varying the price you charge for your good based on (1) whom you are selling it to, (2) how much your customer has already purchased, or (3) when it is purchased.

For an example of case (1), suppose you can segment your customers into two groups: (A) busy and rich customers, and (B) customers with more free time but less income. Group (A) will no doubt have a more *inelastic* demand for your product, meaning that if you raised your price most of these people will continue buying nearly the same amount of your good. In contrast, group (B) will no doubt have a more elastic demand, meaning that you will lose a lot of business from this group if you raise your price. Thus, if you can figure out how to do it, your best strategy to maximize your revenues is to charge a relatively high price to group (A) (since they will keep buying your good anyway) and a relatively low price to group (B) (since this may increase your sales substantially). You can use various tricks to pull this off. For example, offering coupons or rebates is a way of charging your group (B) customers less than your group (A) customers. Busy, wealthy people's *opportunity cost* of time is too high for many of them to spend time cutting coupons or filling out and mailing rebate forms.

You also may be able to increase your revenues by price discriminating based on the quantity of your good your customers purchase or when your customers purchase your good. For example, an ice cream store owner may charge $2 for one scoop but only $3 for two scoops. She knows that consumers' willingness to pay for a second scoop is typically much less than for the first scoop because consumers get *diminishing marginal utility* or less additional satisfaction from consuming additional scoops. By pricing double scoops less than twice the price of single scoops, significantly more sales of double scoops may be achievable.

A third price discrimination strategy you may be able to use is peak-load pricing. Peak-load pricing involves charging higher prices during peak periods to avoid capacity constraints. For example, movie theaters typically offer matinee discounts, since many seats would otherwise remain empty during the day. Theaters also often refuse to accept passes or discount coupons during evenings when new releases are playing, to avoid the theater's capacity constraint.

To summarize, if you have some monopoly power over your product or service, you should carefully explore opportunities to increase your revenues by employing price discrimination strategies. However, if your good can be resold, you may be out of luck. For example, if you give a big discount to your low-income consumers, they might turn around and resell your product to your rich consumers, thereby making profits and depriving you of high priced sales. (The next time you buy ice cream with a friend, rather than each of you buying a single scoop, ask your friend what flavor they want, buy two scoops, and happily divide your scoops and your savings.)

21. Hiring Employees

Once again, the general rule when deciding how much to do any activity is to continue doing the activity as long as the additional (or *marginal*) benefits of the activity exceed the additional (or *marginal*) costs. When the additional benefits no longer exceed the additional costs, stop the activity. To apply this general rule to the questions of how many workers to employ and how many hours to employ each worker, you must estimate the additional benefits and additional costs associated with hiring.

For example, what would be your marginal benefits and marginal costs of hiring another worker for another day? Your marginal cost is simply the daily wage you would pay the worker. [This assumes you don't drive up wage rates by hiring another worker. If you do, your marginal cost of hiring another worker would exceed the wage you would pay this worker.] Estimating your marginal benefit is less straightforward. You will need to estimate the additional revenues (or *marginal revenue product*) the worker would generate for your business. A worker's marginal revenue product equals the extra output (or *marginal product*) your worker produces times the *marginal revenue* (or product price if you sell in a competitive market) you obtain from selling this extra output. You also should keep in mind the principle of *diminishing returns*. At some point, if you hire additional workers (or the same workers for additional hours), your workers' marginal product (and marginal revenue product) will likely fall. Therefore, you should continue hiring only as long as marginal revenue product is greater than the wage paid. It follows that you should not pay a worker an amount greater than the worker's marginal revenue product.

Thus, economic theory provides a framework for deciding whether to hire someone and at what wage to hire them. But when faced with a hiring decision, you still must perform the difficult task of assessing the marginal product the potential employee can generate for your business. This task is difficult because of *asymmetric information*. Job candidates know more about their strengths, weaknesses, and overall productivity than do their potential employers. How do you as an employer assess the likelihood that a job candidate would be a productive employee for your business?

Beyond evaluating obvious factors such as the candidate's related work experience and education, below are a few tips about what else you might consider. First, it may be possible for you to learn something about a job candidate's likely productivity through certain *signals* sent by the candidate that may have nothing to do with the candidate's job specific qualifications. Examples include (1) a candidate who earned high grades from a rigorous college program may signal general competence, even if the degree they earned is unrelated to the work they would be performing; (2) a candidate who appears enthusiastic may signal that they will enjoy and work hard at their job, but a candidate that appears "overly eager" may be signaling that they can't find or keep a job elsewhere, perhaps because they are not as productive as their paper qualifications appear; (3) a candidate who is impeccably dressed may signal attention to detail, or possibly a willingness to waste time on superficial activities. Obviously, interpreting signals is a challenge. Nevertheless, certain signals may provide helpful clues to help you select productive employees.

Another factor to consider when evaluating a job candidate is a candidate's references, but perhaps only references obtained from people you know. The value of references is severely limited because of a *prisoner's dilemma* problem facing those who write references. For example, recommendation letters would be very useful if they were consistently unbiased and frank. But everyone, including employers, knows that most recommendation letters are biased positively. Knowing this, those writing recommendation letters are forced to write increasingly glowing recommendation letters just to meet employers' expectations. Thus, it is unlikely you will learn anything negative about a job candidate by reading (or talking to) their references. However, if you know and periodically communicate with the person providing a reference, you are much more likely to obtain more objective information about the job candidate. The cost of exaggeration, in terms of lost credibility, is much higher to someone you know than to someone you will never meet.

22. Managing Employees

Once you have hired employees, you need to manage them effectively. An important management challenge is motivating employees to work hard, productively, and in a manner that maximizes your business's profits. There are many managerial leadership books available that can help you with certain aspects of this task. Our focus here is on providing the right *incentives* to induce your employees to serve your business as effectively as they can.

Business owners and workers typically have different objectives. Owners wish to maximize profits. Workers wish to maximize their personal interests, including interests such as maximizing their salaries, minimizing their work effort, maximizing their perks, etc. Thus, your workers will pursue their own goals, even if that means less profit for you. The trick for you as a business owner or manager is to use incentives to align, as much as possible, employee behavior that maximizes your profits with employee behavior that best serves employees' interests.

If you can easily monitor your employees' behavior and measure your employees' contributions to your profits, you need only reward workers (through pay or possibly via other means) in accordance with the extra profits they generate for your business. In this way your workers will be motivated to maximize your profits. In most businesses, however, monitoring the productivity of workers is difficult and costly. It may be infeasible for you to know with any degree of certainty the value of the productivity each of your workers generates. If you can't measure your workers' productivity, a second best approach would be for you to measure and reward your workers' efforts. For example, hours worked could be used as an indicator of effort. But effort also may be difficult or costly to measure accurately. Typically, your employees will be much better informed about their effort than you will be. Thus, if you can't closely monitor your employees' behavior, a *principle-agent problem* will occur. When not monitored, your workers (the agents) will pursue their own goals rather than your (the principle's) goal. What can you do?

There is no absolute solution to this principal-agent problem that faces owners and managers who cannot closely monitor their employees. But even when monitoring workers is infeasible, there are ways to offer incentives to promote worker productivity. One way is to develop an incentive structure that rewards the outcome of high worker effort. For example, you could offer revenue-sharing or bonus-payments to your workers based on the profits your business earns each year. This approach may work well for very small businesses where each employee's efforts have a significant impact on the profits of the business and, thus, on the bonus or revenue share they would receive. However, in a large company where each individual worker's efforts have only a very small impact on company profits, revenue sharing and bonus-payment systems may provide insufficient incentive to be effective.

Another incentive strategy you might use to motivate your workers when they cannot be closely monitored is to pay them more than the going market wage and to threaten dismissal if they are caught "shirking." By making the jobs you offer more attractive than other job opportunities available to your employees, you can increase the *opportunity cost* to your employees for getting caught working at a low effort level and being fired. That is, to avoid the risk of losing a good job, your workers may work harder than they otherwise would. Of course, this strategy will be profitable only when the extra worker productivity it generates more than compensates for the extra wages you would have to pay your workers.

Finally, besides motivating workers, another important employee management task worth including in this lesson is the assignment of duties among workers. When deciding how to assign work among employees, you should keep in mind the advantages of specialization and the principle of *comparative advantage*. The principle of comparative advantage states that a task should be assigned to whoever has the lowest opportunity cost of completing the task. By having each employee specialize in performing only those tasks for which they have comparative advantage in performing, more of all tasks can be completed.

For example, suppose you manage or own a small restaurant and hire two employees, Ann and Dave, to perform cooking and cleaning duties. One option would be to split the cooking and cleaning work evenly between your two employees, but this would be inefficient. If Ann cooked faster than Dave and Dave cleaned faster than Ann, then obviously it would make most sense for you to assign cooking to Ann and cleaning to Dave. But what if Ann could cook *and* clean faster than Dave? Should you assign both tasks to Ann? You should not assign both tasks to Ann because there are only so many hours that Ann can work and because Dave would have nothing to do. (You may be able to employ Ann for more hours than Dave, but you might have to pay Ann overtime wages and at some point her productivity would be subject to *diminishing returns.*) Instead, you should assign Ann whichever task she has comparative advantage in performing. For example, if Ann can cook three times as fast as Dave but clean only two times as fast as Dave, she would have comparative advantage in cooking. In this case, you should assign cooking to Ann and cleaning to Dave. It is easy to prove that this assignment would accomplish more cooking and more cleaning for your restaurant. Moreover, by having your employees specialize, you may promote task learning and the development of expertise, which may further increase your workers' productivity.

23.   When Should Your Business Be Open?

As an owner or manager of a business, you must decide what weeks of the year, days of the week, and hours of the day to keep your business open. The general rule to apply is to keep your business open as long as the marginal revenues exceed the marginal costs of being open. The key to correctly implementing this rule is to remember to ignore *fixed costs*. Fixed costs are costs that do not vary with the amount of a product or service produced and sold. Examples of fixed costs include insurance, property taxes, executive salaries, rent, etc. If you keep your business open another week, hour, or day, these costs will not change. Fixed costs, therefore, should not be considered in your decision regarding how long to stay open.

For example, suppose you manage a restaurant and you must decide what time to close the restaurant each day. Suppose you currently close the restaurant at 9 P.M., but you are considering whether to stay open an extra hour. How should you make this decision? First, you need to estimate the additional revenues you would receive from keeping your business open until 10 P.M. You might do this by collecting data about sales from similar restaurants that close at 10 P.M. or by experimenting with the 10 P.M. closing time at your restaurant. Then you need to estimate the additional costs of staying open the extra hour. When doing so, you should include only *variable costs* such as the additional labor, supplies, and utilities costs associated with keeping your business open the extra hour. You should ignore fixed costs such as your insurance, property tax, and building rent and maintenance costs. Thus, it may be profitable for you to stay open the extra hour even if your sales fall significantly after 9 P.M. This lesson explains why restaurants, theaters, airlines, etc., may remain open for business during times when most of their seats are empty.

24. How Much Should You Advertise?

Is it wise to advertise? The answer depends on the nature of the competition you face and the characteristics of the demand for your product or service. First, consider the *market structure* or conditions under which you compete when selling your product.

Suppose you compete within a *perfectly competitive* industry where you sell the exact same product or service as numerous competitors. In this case, advertising makes little sense. Since your competitors sell the same product, you cannot use advertising to differentiate your product and take sales away from your competitors. Advertising might increase the market demand for your good, but almost all of any increase in market sales would go to your competitors. (Moreover, within a perfectly competitive market, firms already can sell as much of their good as they want at the market price.) Advertising would simply raise your costs. This is why you rarely see advertising in highly competitive markets, such as in the markets for agricultural products. (How many tomato commercials have you seen?)

Suppose instead you have monopoly power over your product or service. If you are a pure *monopolist*, you have no competitors to take sales away from through advertising. But you still may wish to advertise so as to increase demand for your good. If instead, as is much more likely the case, you sell within a *monopolistically competitive* or *oligopolistic* market where you have competitors who sell a similar but in some way different good, you will own some degree of monopoly power and the probability that advertising will increase your profits would be higher. Advertising may be essential for increasing the demand for your good by highlighting the advantages to consumers of buying your particular good versus your competitors' goods. Moreover, you may be faced with a *prisoner's dilemma* problem, which will require you to advertise in response to your competitors' advertising (for an example of this problem and how it may be avoided, see Lesson 76).

So, if you own some monopoly power you may benefit from advertising. But how much should you advertise? Once again you should apply the general rule for deciding how much to do any activity—continue doing the activity as long as the additional (or *marginal*) benefits of the activity exceed the additional (or *marginal*) costs. The challenge in this context is to estimate the marginal revenue and marginal cost associated with advertising your good. One common mistake to avoid is justifying advertising by comparing the estimated revenue from increased sales (your marginal benefit) with the cost of the advertising. Advertising leads to increased production and increased production costs. The additional production cost should be added to the advertising costs to compute the full marginal cost of advertising.

To estimate marginal revenue you would receive from advertising, you may first need to implement market surveys or other market research techniques to learn how the demand for your product depends on both the amount of advertising you perform and the price you charge. In general, you should advertise a lot if the demand for your product is very sensitive to advertising and not very sensitive to price. As explained above, the demand for your good is likely to be more sensitive to advertising if there are competitors selling similar but not identical goods. In this case, relatively large advertising expenditures may be justified. If the demand for your good is not sensitive to price (that is, your product has an *inelastic demand*), your markup of price over marginal cost will be large (see Lesson 20). Thus, the profit from each additional sale you make will be large, justifying higher advertising expenditures.

In practice, because of the difficulty of estimating full demand and marginal revenue curves and the impact of advertising expenditures on marginal revenue, it may be difficult for managers to apply the marginal revenue versus marginal cost rule to precisely determine the profit maximizing level of advertising. So, based on the marginal revenue versus marginal cost rule, economists have developed a rule of thumb for advertising that requires only estimates of the price and advertising *elasticity of demand*. This rule of thumb states that to maximize profit on sales of any good, a manager's advertising to sales ratio should equal the ratio of the advertising and price elasticities. For example, suppose your business's total revenues equal $100,000 and you spend $2,000 on advertising (so that your advertising to sales ratio equals $2,000/$100,000, or 2 percent). Suppose through market research you estimate that a 50% increase in advertising would lead to a 10% increase in sales (so that your product has an advertising elasticity of demand equal to 10%/50%, or 0.2). Suppose you also estimate that a 10% increase in your product's price will lead to a 50% loss in sales (so that your product has a price elasticity of demand equal to 50%/10%, or 5). It follows that to maximize profits, your advertising to sales ratio should be 0.2/5, or 4 percent. Thus, you should increase your advertising budget from $2,000 to $4,000.

25.   When Should You Close Your Business?

As long as your business can make *economic profit,* it will make sense for you to keep your business open. For a one-product business, economic profit equals total revenue [price (P) × quantity sold (Q)] minus total cost (TC), where total cost includes all *opportunity costs* associated with producing and selling the product. So if P × Q > TC, stay open. Or, dividing both sides of this equation by Q, if P > TC/Q stay open, where TC/Q is the *average total cost* or per unit cost of producing and selling your product.

But should you ever keep your business open when P falls below average total cost and you are not making economic profit? There are least two circumstances where you should not close your business even though you are losing money.

First, in the short term, you should keep your business open if you can cover your *variable costs* (that is, if P > average variable cost) even if you cannot cover your total costs. This is true because you should always ignore your *sunk costs* when deciding whether to close your business. For example, suppose you opened a small business as an independent truck driver. On January 1 you signed a 1-year lease for $4,000 for your truck. You estimated that each roundtrip job also will cost you $200 in fuel, maintenance, and time costs, that the price you will receive per job will equal $250, and that you will be able to complete 100 jobs over the course of the year. Thus, you expected an annual economic profit of $1,000 (($250 – $200) × 100 jobs – $4,000). However, on January 2, suppose the market price fell to $225 per job. Thus, if you don't close your business, your economic profit for the year will equal –$1,500 (($225 – $200) × 100 jobs – $4,000). Nevertheless, you should not close your business, since the price still exceeds your variable costs ($200) per job. The $4,000 cost to lease your truck is a sunk cost. It has already been paid and cannot be recovered by shutting down your business. Thus, this cost should be ignored when deciding whether to close. Looked at another way, if you close your business on January 2, you will lose $4,000, but if you continue your business for a year, you will lose only $1,500. Of course, you should shut down your business at the end of the year rather than spend another $4,000 to lease another truck.

Another situation when you may not want to close your business even though you are losing money is when you expect the *demand* for your product to increase (or the cost to produce your product to decrease) in the future. For example, you may believe it will take time for consumers to learn about your product. Thus, you may accept short-run losses until demand for your product increases. Alternatively, you might expect demand for your product to increase in the future if you sell a product subject to *network externalities*. Network externalities occur when the demand for a product increases as more people own the product (or as the network gets bigger). For example, telephones would be of little value if few people owned them. Thus, you may eventually profit by staying in business even while losing money if demand for your product increases after more people own the product. Indeed, capturing network externalities may be one of the few ways to achieve and maintain monopoly power and profits (as demonstrated by Microsoft though sales of its windows operating system).

In some cases it may be most profitable for you to shut down your business and then reopen after demand has increased or production costs have fallen. But often there are costs associated with shutting down or starting up a business. If these costs are large, you may need to stay open to achieve long-run profits. But remember, because of the *opportunity cost* associated with interest (see Lesson 17), future profits should not be weighed equally with up front losses. A $1 loss today would require at least a $1 \times (1 + \text{interest rate})$ profit next year to be worth incurring.

Finally, by using the lessons of economics to help you profitably run your business, you may be able to avoid having to consider the question of when you should close your business.

PART TWO:
USING ECONOMICS TO UNDERSTAND
THE WORLD

Introduction

In addition to using economics to make better decisions, you can use economics to understand the world around you. Misconceptions about the world are everywhere. Some of these misconceptions initiate from general ignorance, others from emotional and muddied thinking, and still others are created via deceptive but effective business advertising or political rhetoric. As a result, people are sometimes fooled into making decisions about what to buy, who to vote for, or how to live that do not serve their best interests or the interests of others. But with an economic microscope in hand, you can see through many of these misconceptions. To use economics to dispel myths, understand and predict human behavior, and evaluate public policies, I recommend you begin by following these three basic rules:

Rule 1: Be a critical thinker: Require sound reasons before believing.

Humans are hard-wired to be emotional. Emotions, as well as biases due to our own personal desires, situation, or history, can distort our view of the world. If you want to see the world through clear and unfiltered glasses, you will need to avoid these common biases. Form opinions by carefully thinking, not by impulsively feeling. Discipline yourself to keep asking, "Why?" until sufficient evidence or logical reasons are presented. Only then should you believe. Economics takes this logical, scientific approach to understanding. But even the best scientist is not completely objective (except perhaps Mr. Spock from the old Star Trek series), but this fact does not prevent you from being as rational and objective as you can be. Only in this way will you come closest to understanding the world.

Rule 2:   Study the incentives facing people.

Human behavior is mostly understandable and predictable. Humans respond to *incentives*. Incentives affect the costs and benefits people face when making decisions. Thus, incentives affect the decisions people make. Indeed, incentives drive human behavior. By identifying and understanding the incentives facing people, you will be prepared to explain and predict their behavior.

Rule 3:   Look and think beyond the obvious.

The world is not always simple. Sometimes what appears obvious is not. To avoid being fooled, it is often necessary to look and think beyond obvious initial effects and to consider less obvious secondary (and often unintended) consequences of decisions and policies. Often these secondary effects can be understood or predicted using straightforward economic analysis of how the incentives people face have changed or will change as a result of decisions or policies. Thus, to understand the world, you will need to think objectively, carefully, and critically. But you also will need to look beyond the obvious and sometimes "outside the box" for answers.

To illustrate how to use this advice to see the world more clearly, consider the following public policy question:

Do minimum wage laws help low-income families?

Minimum (or living) wage laws require employers to pay their workers some minimum hourly wage rate. The obvious purpose of these laws is to help low-income families. But do they? Let's apply our three rules:

Rule 1: When I ask my students this question, they quickly and nearly unanimously answer, "Yes, of course." My students care about low-income families (many of them are members of low-income families). They "feel" that low-income families (perhaps like their own) deserve a break. But to understand the world, we must think critically or else risk being fooled. We must demand logical reasons and/or empirical evidence before jumping to conclusions.

Rule 2: People respond to incentives. When employers are made to give raises to their low-wage workers, their incentive to hire low-wage workers will be reduced. Thus, they will likely hire less low-wage workers. With less workers and the requirement to pay some workers higher salaries, some employers might close their business, others may raise their product prices and sell less of their products.

Rule 3: By examining how this policy affects the incentives facing people, the unintended impacts from the policy can be identified. High minimum wages will increase unemployment, especially for low-skilled workers—the socioeconomic group these laws are intended to help. Also, higher consumer prices may burden low-income families.

Finally, data indicate that many workers who benefit from minimum wage laws are teenagers who live in above-average-income families. Thus, these laws do not direct aid to low-income families efficiently. Might there be better ways to help low-income families, ways that don't create unemployment, higher consumer prices, and income gains to families who are not in need?

This analysis does not prove minimum wage laws are mistakes. But it clearly illustrates why it is important to look and think beyond the obvious. By thinking logically, considering empirical evidence, examining how a policy affects the incentives facing people, and using this knowledge to identify secondary consequences, the merit of this and other policies can be objectively assessed.

Part Two of this book provides numerous examples of how you can apply these and other basic economic ideas to help you dispel myths, solve apparent paradoxes, understand why things are as they are, and sort through political spin and conventional thought to understand and evaluate important public policies.

CHAPTER 3:
Dispel Myths and Detect Bologna:
Common Fallacies that Need Debunking

Introduction

This chapter is about identifying and dispelling common myths and misconceptions. I'm sure you've heard and may believe at least some of the fallacies tested in this chapter. They are repeated over and over again via media reports and everyday conversations. Some are mainly curiosities. Others are critically important to peoples' lives. All of the fallacies debunked in this chapter involve valuable lessons.

26.   Economics Is About Money

When I ask my students on the first day of economics class to describe in a few words what economics is about I usually hear the same words—money, business, the stock market, and a few others. All of these items are a part of economics, but economics is much broader in its scope, application, and importance. In fact, economics is largely about how to obtain and promote happiness. Is there anything more important than this?

Definitions of economics vary, but most textbook definitions say something like—"Economics is the study of how people choose to use their limited resources in their attempt to satisfy their wants." There is no mention of money in this definition or in any textbook definition I have ever seen. Indeed, many economic decisions and questions do not involve money at all. Economics is about how individuals, businesses, and governments make decisions to achieve their goals. It is also about understanding our world better so that we can make our world better. Economics is everywhere and all-important to our lives.

This book attempts to show you how economics can be used to help you achieve happiness for yourself and for others.

27.   Money Is the Key to Happiness

Since economics is largely about happiness, economists have begun to investigate the sources of human happiness. In particular, they have begun to study the degree to which income and wealth determine a person's happiness. Although the final verdict is not in, evidence is mounting that money is not usually a strong determinant of happiness. For example, surveys indicate that: (1) the U.S. population does not report feeling happier over the last several decades despite rising *real* incomes, (2) people living in wealthy countries report feeling only a little happier than people living in less wealthy countries, and (3) lottery winners claim not to be significantly happier one year after winning the lottery than before winning. In contrast to this evidence, survey results also suggest that income is strongly related to the happiness of low-income individuals. Thus, money may be the key to happiness, but only for people who have very little of it.

These preliminary findings are consistent with the economic principle of *diminishing marginal utility of income.* For example, if you make $200,000 per year, how much more happiness does another $1,000 bring you? If you are relatively wealthy, another $1,000 probably wouldn't matter much to your life. But if you made $10,000 per year, an extra $1,000 could be used to buy relative necessities that may make you significantly happier. Thus, it seems that if someone's basic needs are not being met, then giving them money, or at least giving them opportunities to earn money, may be the best way to raise their happiness. But for people whose basic needs are already met, the key to happiness may need to be found elsewhere.

28.   Poverty Has Been Eliminated in the United States

Many college students believe that poverty in America is a problem only to be studied in U.S. history classes. But poverty continues within America. The U.S. government defines the poverty line by estimating a minimum food budget per family and multiplying this number by three. Families with income below this line are defined as living in poverty. As last calculated in 2003, the poverty rate in the United States was 12.5%, meaning that roughly people 35 million people are living in poverty in America. Despite considerable economic growth, the U.S. poverty rate actually rose (from 11.1% in 1973) over the last three decades. Poverty rates within the United States are highly correlated with race (Blacks and Hispanics, over 20%), family type (single parent females, approximately 25%), and educational attainment (high school dropouts, roughly 25%).

Of course, poverty is a relative concept. Nearly 90% of those living in 1900 in the United States would fall below the poverty line as it is defined today. Moreover, someone considered poor in the United States may be considered quite wealthy within the less developed countries of the world today. Also, the poverty rate as defined by the U.S. government is very simple and imperfect statistic. For example, a medical school student may be considered in poverty while in medical school, even though the expected lifetime earnings of this student would be very high. Still, tens of millions of people are struggling to meet their basic needs, even within the wealthiest country in the world.

29.   War Is Good for an Economy

The first lesson of economics is that we can't have everything we want. Because resources are scare, trade-offs are inevitable and we must make choices. A nation must choose between employing its labor, capital, and natural resources toward the production of guns (military goods) or employing its resources toward the production of butter (domestic goods). If the federal government employs workers, machines, and raw materials to produce army tanks, the *opportunity cost* will be less workers, machines, and raw materials available in the private sector to produce automobiles.

World War II is frequently cited as an example of how war can help an economy. Historians have observed that military spending during World War II stimulated the U.S. economy and helped bring the United States out of the depression economy of the 1930s. War spending can and, no doubt coincidentally, did serve as effective expansionary *fiscal policy* during the 1940s. Moreover, because unemployment was high and industry was not producing near full capacity at the beginning of the World War II build-up, it was possible to produce more military goods without *crowding out* an equal amount of private sector goods from the U.S. economy. That is, more guns could be produced without giving up that much more butter, because a lot of resources were idle and not being used to produce butter.

Nevertheless, spending for World War II did crowd out private-sector consumption and business investment spending to some degree. Thus, the standard of living in the United States fell during the war years. The war spending also created considerable debt. Further, even during times when expansionary fiscal policy may be called for, numerous other government spending options, such as spending on education, health care, or public infrastructure could be chosen to stimulate the economy at least as effectively as war spending. Perhaps the biggest economic benefit uniquely attributable to World War II was that the national crisis created by this war inspired an increase in the size and *worker productivity* of the U.S. labor force. Undoubtedly, this same inspirational effect on U.S. productivity has not reoccurred during more modern day, less critical wars.

Finally, wars have been disastrous for the economies of many of the less developed countries around the world. All too often, dictators have squandered their country's very limited resources fighting wars instead of caring for the enormous needs of their population. While the benefits of war may at times exceed the costs, waging war consumes human and physical resources well beyond the human and property losses inflicted by the enemy.

30.   Automation and New Technologies Cost the U.S. Jobs

It is widely believed that industry adoption of computers, machines, robots, and other automation technologies is a major cause of unemployment. But new technologies are likely to create more jobs than they destroy.

To understand how machines that replace workers create jobs, consider the following. Engineers are currently developing robots that will one day be used on a large scale to automate home construction at a low production cost per house. The adoption of this new technology will cause home construction workers to lose their jobs. But this new technology will create jobs too. First, the operation, maintenance, and upgrading of the computerized robots may require more computer programmers and engineers to be hired. (Consider the huge industry and number of jobs the invention of the computer created.) Second, the new technology will reduce the cost of building homes. Lower production costs will lead to lower home prices. Lower home prices will lead to more sales. But more home sales will lead to more sales of *complementary goods* such as furniture, appliances, and other products, creating jobs in these industries. Perhaps most importantly, lower home prices mean consumers will have more money left over after buying a home to spend elsewhere, thereby creating jobs throughout the economy. Finally, profits in the home construction industry may increase and lead to greater business investment or other spending, which may create even more jobs.

There is plenty of empirical evidence that new technologies needn't reduce employment. Consider agriculture. At the beginning of the 20th century, roughly 40% of U.S. workers worked on a farm. Because of the use of labor-saving agricultural technologies, the need to employ farm workers has declined dramatically. Today less than 2% of the U.S. workforce is employed on a farm. Yet, overall employment is much higher and the unemployment rate is lower today than it was in 1900. Technological advances in agricultural production shifted employment away from the agricultural sector, but these advances helped create jobs in other sectors of the economy. Similarly, over the last several years, new technologies eliminated manufacturing and clerical jobs in the United States. But overall employment increased as many more professional, managerial, and service sector jobs were created.

There is no shortage of work that can be undertaken. Thus, there is no limit to the number of jobs an economy can support. New technologies may displace workers, but they also create jobs and raise standards of living.

31. Immigration Costs the U.S. Jobs

A common belief is that immigrants steal American jobs. But this belief, like the belief that machines eliminate jobs, falls victim to the "lump of labor fallacy"—that there are only so many jobs to go around.

Immigrants to the United States may displace U.S. workers in certain industries, but they also create jobs opportunities in other sectors of the economy. Immigration increases the *supply* of workers and lowers production costs. Lower production costs lead to greater production, greater business profits, and lower consumer prices. All of these effects from immigration lead to the creation of more jobs. Plus, new immigrants *demand* new goods and services. This demand also creates new jobs.

32. International Trade Costs the U.S. Jobs

Industry cries for protection against foreign competition are frequent and loud. They claim cheap imports destroy American industries and American jobs. But economists have long argued that free trade creates jobs and leads to improved standards of living for all countries that participate (see Lesson 101).

If countries specialize in the production of products and services they have *comparative advantage* in producing and then trade with each other, all countries benefit. Consider a real world example. Suppose the United States has comparative advantage in producing pharmaceuticals and Mexico has comparative advantage in producing clothing. It would be easy to show that both countries could obtain more of both goods if the United States specialized in the production of drugs and exported some to Mexico and Mexico specialized in the production of clothing and exported some to the United States. This trade, however, will hurt the U.S. textile industry (and the Mexican pharmaceuticals industry) and cause job losses. But it will also create jobs in the U.S. pharmaceutical industry (and the Mexican textile industry). Plus, with more drugs and more clothing *supplied*, the prices of these products will fall. This will free up money for consumers, which they can then spend on other goods or services, thereby creating more jobs throughout the economy.

Or consider an extreme hypothetical example. Suppose another country was willing to produce all the cars we want in exchange for a penny each! Accepting cars from this charitable country would cause considerable job losses in the U.S. auto industry. So should we refuse the offer? Of course we shouldn't. Accepting the free cars would free labor and capital resources currently employed in the auto industry for use elsewhere in the economy. More goods and services (other than cars which we would already have enough of) would be produced and consumed in the United States. Thus, our standard of living would improve. Moreover, since we no longer would need to pay for our cars, we would have much more income available to spend on other goods and services. This spending would create many more jobs.

33.   Outsourcing of Work Costs the U.S. Jobs

In early 2004, the new Chairman of President Bush's Council of Economic Advisors, Gregory Mankiw, got in a whole lot of political trouble when he suggested in widely publicized remarks that the outsourcing of U.S. jobs to other countries may actually be a good thing for the United States. While his statements were considered a political blunder by most everyone, Dr. Mankiw's remarks made perfectly good economic sense.

Outsourcing of jobs is just another form of international trade. Instead of trade in goods and services, outsourcing is trade in labor. Outsourcing occurs, for example, when a U.S. company decides to employ foreign workers (who may be living thousands of miles away) instead of U.S. workers. The initial effect of outsourcing, obviously, is lost U.S. jobs within the industry that is outsourcing work (just like the initial impact of trade in goods is lost U.S. jobs in the industry competing with imports). But the less obvious longer run impact on U.S. jobs and the U.S. economy is positive.

First, U.S. businesses outsource work to low-wage workers in foreign countries to reduce labor costs. Lower production costs lead to higher business profits. Higher profits lead to more business investment (which will create more jobs) or greater earnings for owners or stockholders (which will be spent creating more jobs in other industries). Plus, some of the cost savings will be passed to consumers in the form of lower prices, freeing consumer income to be spent elsewhere (which will create more jobs throughout the economy).

Also, outsourcing allows foreign workers (sometimes very poor foreign workers) to earn U.S. dollars. Eventually, these dollars will be used to buy U.S. goods, services, or assets. Thus, when foreigners earn more U.S. dollars they may import more goods and services from the United States (which will create more jobs in U.S. export industries).

Ultimately, while specific worker groups may be harmed by outsourcing, the overall impact of free trade in labor markets is greater production, more goods and services available for all countries, and greater employment overall.

Dr. Mankiw has since left his position in the Bush Administration to return to Harvard University. Let's hope future advisors to the President demonstrate at least as much courage by speaking the truth even when the truth is unpopular.

34.   Sweat Shops Exploit Workers in Poor Countries

It may be hard for many Americans to accept, but for many people living in less developed countries, even a very hard, very low-paying "sweatshop" job is much better than no job at all. Many millions of people struggle every day to obtain the basic necessities of life for themselves and their families. For them, a job of almost any kind is an opportunity for survival. They choose to work long hours in unsafe conditions for very low pay, because the alternative (having no income) is worse. It may seem humane to include labor rights requirements within trade agreements that require all workers to be provided safe working conditions and minimum wages. But doing so would raise employers' costs of employing workers. Employers would respond by hiring fewer workers and possibly by going out of business. The elimination of work opportunities would end up hurting many of the people such labor rights requirements are intended to help. This would be inhumane.

Trade is good for workers in poor countries. Since poor countries have a *comparative advantage* in producing labor-intensive products, trade generates many jobs in these countries. While incredibly low-paying by U.S. standards, export jobs often pay significantly higher wages than elsewhere within poor countries. Export industries also create competition for labor, which drives up wage rates throughout these countries. Trade may provide a way out of poverty, as it did for various Asian countries such as Hong Kong, Singapore, South Korea, and Taiwan.

There is an exception, however, to the principle that work must benefit workers—when the work is involuntary. Forced prisoner or child labor, for example, is slavery and obviously need not serve these laborers. Clearly, there is good reason to prohibit such practices within trade agreements.

35.   Trade Deficits Are a Sign of a Weak Economy

A *trade deficit* occurs when a country's *imports* exceed their *exports*. For example, when the United States spends more buying goods and services from other countries than it receives in revenue on sales of goods and services to other countries, it runs a trade deficit. On the surface, such a "deficit" sounds like bad news. But consider why trade deficits, such as those typically run in the United States, occur.

First, trade deficits may occur in a country when the country's economy is growing more rapidly than their trading partners' economies. If the economy in the United States is booming, but the rest of the world's economies are depressed, consumers in the United States will have extra income to buy imports, while consumers in the rest of the world will not be able to afford goods produced in the United States. These effects may cause the United States to run a trade deficit.

Alternatively, trade deficits may occur because of financial capital flows. For example, suppose the United States is considered a good place to invest because the economy is expected to grow. In this case, the United States will experience a *capital inflow* (money coming into the United States to buy U.S. assets). This must be accompanied by an increase in the *demand* for U.S. dollars (needed to buy U.S. assets), which will likely cause an increase in the *exchange rate* of the U.S. dollar. This appreciation of the U.S. dollar will make imports cheaper for U.S. consumers and U.S. exports more expensive for foreign buyers. The result may be higher trade deficits in the United States.

Thus, trade deficits are not a sign of a weak economy. In contrast, trade deficits typically occur in countries that are experiencing strong economic growth and providing investment opportunities that attract foreign investors.

36.   Running Up the National Debt Must Burden Future Generations

When the U.S. government spends more money than it takes in through taxes (as it usually does), it runs a budget *deficit*. Each year the federal government runs a budget deficit it increases the *national debt*. It is generally assumed that increasing the national debt will burden our children and grandchildren. But this need not be the case.

First, most money borrowed by the U.S. government is borrowed from within the United States. A rising national debt means U.S. citizens will have to pay higher taxes in the future to pay higher interest on the this debt, but most of this interest will be paid to U.S. citizens (albeit, not the same citizens). Those paying higher taxes and those receiving interest payments will be of the same generation.

Whether or not government borrowing burdens future generations depends on what the government does with the borrowed money. When the government borrows from the private sector, less money is available for consumer and business spending. This burdens the current generation, but it may also burden future generations since less investment spending may mean less consumer goods will be available in the future. For example, less private investment spending on education, capital goods (such as machines, new buildings, etc.), and research and development could lower future productivity, thus making less goods and services available for future generations.

But if the government invests borrowed money intelligently, such as for much needed public infrastructure or other *public goods*, the benefits to future generations from such public investments may exceed the *opportunity cost* of the *crowded out* private sector investments. In this case, future generations will be better off because of the government's decision to borrow and increase the national debt. On the other hand, if the government borrows money to pay for consumption goods and services that provide benefits primarily to the current generation, or worse, to finance wasteful government programs, then future generations will have to pay higher taxes without receiving commensurate benefits.

Even borrowing from foreign sources (*external debt*), which imposes interest payment costs only on future taxpayers, need not burden future generations if the borrowed money is invested productively.

To summarize, just as personal borrowing may or may not improve your economic future, government borrowing may or may not improve the economic future for future generations. Whether or not government borrowing is good for our children and grandchildren depends on whether the borrowed money is invested more productively by the government than it would have otherwise been invested by the private sector.

37.   Contributors to Social Security Eventually Get Their Money Back

The workings of the U.S. Social Security system are much misunderstood. Social Security is a transfer program. The money you contribute (through your payroll taxes) does not come back to you. Instead, your money, along with an equal co-payment from your employer, is transferred to current retirees or other Social Security recipients alive today. When you retire, your Social Security benefits are supposed to be paid through taxes collected from workers (and their employers) at that time.

Okay, so you do not get back the same money you contribute, but do you get back the same amount of money you contributed? Answer: No. The amount of Social Security benefits you will receive will depend on how long you live and various other factors. Surprisingly, it has turned out so far that Social Security recipients have received more than twice the amount of money they and their employers have contributed plus interest!

Because of overly generous benefit formulas and the coming retirement of the baby boom generation (see Lesson 96) the U.S. Social Security system cannot remain solvent indefinitely without "adjustments." While the Social Security system will not go completely broke, college students should not expect the bonanza received by past and current retirees to be available when they retire.

38.   The President Should Get the Credit or Take the Blame for the Economy

The re-election success of first-term U.S. presidents has often been determined, at least in large part, by the state of the nation's economy near the time of the election. But for several reasons, U.S. presidents have very limited influence on the current economy.

First, the most often employed and most important macroeconomic policy tool—*monetary policy*, is not controlled by the president in the United States. The *Federal Reserve* (Fed) controls the money supply and, thus, short-term interest rates throughout the economy. The Fed Chairman (presently Alan Greenspan) and other members of the *Federal Open Market Committee* (FOMC) probably have more influence on the nation's current inflation, unemployment, and economic growth rates than does the president. The FOMC is composed of 7 *Board of Governors* (BOG) and 5 Federal Reserve Bank presidents. A president may appoint a new member of the BOG (subject to congressional confirmation), but terms last 14 years. Thus, most current Fed members were appointed by previous presidents, and the FOMC has a high degree of policy independence.

While the president can influence *fiscal policy* by proposing a national budget (spending and taxation plan), by selling his or her budget priorities to the public, and through veto power, it is Congress that has primary authority over the U.S. budget. Moreover, fiscal policy works with long lags. For example, it typically takes many months to pass a tax cut bill. Then after it is passed, the full impact of the tax cut on the economy may not be fully felt throughout the economy for many months or even years. Thus, the current state of the economy may at times depend more on policies implemented by the previous president than by the actions of the current president. In fact, sometimes policies implemented many years back may be largely responsible for current economic conditions. For example, excessive government spending during the Johnson Administration was the probable cause of inflation that took many years to mitigate. Another good example occurred during the Reagan Administration. The Reagan Administration cut taxes and increased government spending (particularly military spending) which greatly increased the *national debt* and ultimately created budget problems for future administrations.

Finally, events entirely outside of a president's control often cause macroeconomic problems. For example, a *recession* in Europe and Asia could cause an economic slowdown in the

United States since foreign countries would reduce spending on U.S.-made goods. Or consider the oil price shocks that occurred during the Carter Administration. The price of crude oil quadrupled throughout the late 1970s mainly because the Organization of Petroleum Exporting Countries (OPEC) formed a *cartel*, restricted oil exports, and raised prices. This caused both inflation and unemployment in the United States. No one should blame U.S. politicians for such events. But many do. Carter lost his presidency to Reagan.

All this is not to say that presidents have no effect on their economy. Besides influencing budgetary policy, presidents can implement regulatory and trade policies that can have a relatively near-term effect on the economy. Plus, presidents can start wars or implement other non-economic policies that can have macroeconomic consequences. So, presidents can impact the ongoing economy, but not as much as most people think.

39.   Money Is Backed by Gold

Many years ago, the United States was on a gold standard. Paper money could be converted to gold on demand. But today in the United States, and in most other modern nations, money is not backed by anything. Money has little or no intrinsic value. That is, it can't be used for much (except perhaps for wallpaper). So why do people want it so badly?

People work hard to earn money because they expect other people to accept their money in exchange for goods and services. Governments declare their currency "legal tender," but what really gives money its value is the expectation that others will value it.

40.   Money Is Created by Revving Up the Printing Presses

Most people believe that when the U.S. government wants to increase the amount of money flowing through the economy they simply crank up the printing presses and distribute the cash somehow. But the money creation process employed in the United States and other modern economies is really quite different.

First, it is important to realize that currency (paper and coin) is not the only form of money in our economy. Money also includes other assets, such as checking accounts, that can be used on demand to pay for goods and services. Since checks serve the same purpose as cash, they too are money. In fact, the majority of money in the U.S. economy is in the form of accounts held in financial institutions, not currency.

To increase the money supply, the *Federal Reserve* (Fed) writes a check (which is not backed by any explicitly held funds!) to the private sector in exchange for government bonds (which are like IOUs). This check eventually gets deposited in an account in a bank somewhere and thus money is created. But the money creation process does not stop there. The bank receiving this new deposit loans out a large fraction of their new funds (that's how banks make profits). But when banks make loans to individuals or business, these loans are used to purchase goods and services. The sellers of these goods and services get new checks, which end up in their bank accounts. With new accounts created throughout the banking system, new money will have been created.

If the Fed wants to reduce the money supply, they sell bonds and the above process will work in reverse. It is in this way, not through the printing presses, that our government controls the nation's money supply.

41. Inflation Is Bad Because It Raises Everyone's Cost of Living

Inflation is a general rise in prices throughout the economy. It is commonly believed that higher prices are bad because consumers will not be able to afford as many goods and services. This may seem an obvious truth, but it is, in fact, generally false. For example, if prices of all products and services double, business revenues must double. Accordingly, incomes throughout the economy will double. But if prices double and incomes double, *real incomes* will not change. Consumers will be no worse off from the inflation.

Inflation does impose certain costs on certain people. For example, those with significant cash holdings would see the real value of these holdings fall as a result of inflation. But because incomes rise as prices rise, most people are relatively unharmed by moderate inflation. Very high inflation, however, can spiral out of control and severely disrupt a market system (see Lesson 63).

42.   Some Places Are a Lot Better to Live In than Others

"Places rated" guides sell a lot of books. Based on various quality of life factors, they typically compute and provide an overall annual ranking of the "best places to live" in the United States. However, the idea that some places are and will remain much better to live in than other places is shortsighted. For the average person, no place will remain significantly better to live in than any other.

Suppose some city really was a great place to live and that the places rated guides correctly ranked the city #1. Eventually, more people would move to this city. People would continue moving to this city until real estate costs, traffic congestion, pollution, etc., increased to the point where it no longer was desirable to move to the city. Thus, after people had fully migrated, this place would end up no more desirable to move to than any other place. Of course, as explained in Lesson 5, people who have stronger than average preferences for a particular attribute of a location, such as good weather, may be happier living in San Diego indefinitely. But they would pay for this preference with higher housing costs, etc. Meanwhile, people of relatively low income might prefer a lower-cost place to live. But, for people of average preferences, no place will remain better overall to live in than any other.

The reason why the same places tend to rank high year after year in the places rated guides may have less to do with how desirable it is to live in these places and more to do with the somewhat arbitrary selection and weighting of the factors employed in these studies.

43. Manufacturers Make Products that Wear Out So They Can Sell More

Why can't tennis ball manufacturers make tennis balls that last all summer? Some people believe the answer is that they can but they choose not to. After all, some may argue, if they sold tennis balls that didn't wear out all summer, they would reduce their sales of tennis balls to one can per summer.

This reasoning, however, is false. If tennis ball manufacturers could make tennis balls that lasted ten times longer, they would as long as it cost them less than ten times as much to do so. For example, suppose the cost to make a can of tennis balls is $2 and competition has driven the price of a can down to $2. Now suppose Wilson invents a new manufacturing process that allows them to produce tennis balls that would last ten times as long, but that this process would cost Wilson five times as much. Wilson could produce the longer-life balls and sell them for as much as $20 per can. As long as the price of these longer-life balls was no more than $20 per can, consumers (assuming they believe the balls will last ten times as long) would buy them since the price per use time is no more than with the $2 per can balls. Wilson would sell the new balls and make as much as $10 per longer-life can sold. Eventually, Penn, Dunlap, etc., may learn how to make the longer-life balls and start selling them. Such competition would drive down the price of these longer-life cans, benefiting consumers at the expense of Wilson's profits. But in the meantime, Wilson would have made profits that they otherwise wouldn't have made. The bottom line is that if longer-life products can be cost effectively produced, they will be. Sellers will make up for lost sales by raising prices.

44.   It Is Fairer to Tax Corporations than People

Business taxes may be more politically popular than taxes directly imposed on individuals, but one way or another, people pay taxes. Moreover, just because business owners or corporate executives are made to pay taxes to the government does not mean that these individuals bear most of the burden of such taxes. In some cases, the burden may fall much more on low-income individuals.

When a corporation or other form of business is made to pay a tax, the business will respond to the tax by (1) cutting dividend payments to shareholders (if the business is a corporation) or profits to the business owners, (2) reducing output and cutting costs, such as by reducing wages paid and/or the number of workers hired, (3) closing their business, or (4) raising their product prices.

Businesses would like to pass taxes along to consumers in the form of higher prices. All else equal, when the demand for an industry's product is highly *inelastic*, businesses within the industry can simply raise the price of their product and consumers will continue to buy nearly as much of the product as before. In this case, it is consumers, not those from the affected industry, that bear the burden of the taxes paid by the industry. Gasoline taxes, for example, primarily burden gasoline consumers, not the gasoline industry. So it is low-income consumers, not wealthy business executives that are harmed most by some business taxes. In other cases, for example, when the demand for an industry's product is highly *elastic*, businesses within the industry can't simply increase the price of their product because consumers will buy much less of the product if they do. But even in these cases, the losers may be primarily lower-income workers. If industry sales fall, fewer workers will be demanded and wages and employment will fall.

Whether they ultimately impact consumers, shareholders, and/or workers, people bear the burden of taxes on corporations. Many of these people may be of lower income.

45. Monopolies Charge Any Price They Want and Are Always Bad

Do monopolies rip us off? Like all businesses, monopolies try to maximize their profits. Because monopolies do not have competitors, they may be able to set the price of their product or service high, above their *average cost* of production, thereby making (potentially large) profits. Consumers bear the burden of these higher prices. However, monopolies can't charge any price they want. They face a downward sloping *demand* for their product or service. If they raise their price too high, their sales and profits will fall. Just because there is only one seller does not mean buyers must pay any price the monopolist sets. Consumers may choose not to buy at all.

In some cases, monopolies may charge lower prices than would be charged if the industry was composed of numerous smaller competitors. Some industries experience *economies of scale*. Economies of scale occur when a business can reduce their average production costs by increasing the quantity of what they produce. This may occur because of the opportunity for large companies to employ specialized workers or because some production inputs must be purchased no matter how many products or services are produced (see Lesson 19). Thus, a large *natural monopoly* may be able to produce at much lower cost and sell its product at a lower price than would occur if the industry was competitive.

Monopolies, therefore, are not always bad for consumers. In fact, sometimes our government purposely creates monopolies! For example, our government may issue a patent to a pharmaceutical company on a drug they have newly developed. The patent gives the company the exclusive legal right to sell their drug for a number of years. Until the patent expires, the company selling the drug has a monopoly in the market for that particular drug. As a result, the price of the patented drug may be set high. But if patent protection were impossible, the company probably would not have poured money into research and development to produce the drug in the first place (since after sale the drug could be copied and sold by competitors). The opportunity to make monopoly profits provides a powerful *incentive* for businesses to innovate and develop new products. This too is good for consumers.

So, monopolies may rip us off, but they are not always undesirable.

46.   Saving One Life Is Worth Any Cost

The idea that we can never be too safe is overly simplistic. Safety is not free. Inevitably, people face trade-offs between reducing the risk of physical harm and other things they value. We all face such trade-offs every day when we walk across the street, drive our cars, eat junk food, etc. We choose to accept a certain amount of risk of injury, illness, or death in order to obtain things we want.

Governments also face trade-offs between saving lives and providing other goods and services that are valued. Policies with the sole objective of saving as many lives as possible would *not* serve the public interest. For example, our government could eliminate airline accident fatalities by banning all flights or by making safety requirements so extreme and costly that no one could afford a ticket. Or consider air pollution. Certain air pollutants increase the risk of premature mortality. Should all air pollution be eliminated? To do so would require that we ban automobiles, shut down factories, stop using electricity, and enormously reduce our standard of living. Indeed, such a policy would wreck our economy, create massive unemployment, and result in more lives lost due to poverty than would have been lost due to pollution.

To summarize, there is a cost of reducing risks. Even when it is possible to reduce risks that could save lives, it may not be preferable to do so. Decisions regarding safety, like with all decisions, should be made by weighing expected benefits and costs.

47.   The Right to Freedom Is Inalienable and Priceless

The assertion that people should somehow be granted absolute "rights" is bad economics. We all may place a very high value on certain qualities of life such as freedom. But the provision of freedom is not costless, and the value of freedom is not infinite.

Consider, for example, a few of the "rights" defined in the U.S. Bill of Rights. While freedom of speech may be highly desirable, sometimes the *opportunity cost* of such freedom is not worth paying. Most people agree, for example, that the freedom to yell "fire" in a movie theater or to discuss military secrets or the construction of weapons of mass destruction in public would entail too great a cost to be justified. Or consider the "right" to be protected from searches and seizures. In our world today, complete protection may increase the risk of successful terrorism and, thus, may not be worth the cost. Or consider the "right" to keep and bear arms. Does this mean that everyone should have the "right" to own and carry a machine gun? (Will those who insist machine gun ownership is an absolute "right", be willing to pay higher taxes to pay for machine guns for people who can't afford to buy one? Not likely.)

There are many other examples of so-called "rights" that are often cited as being absolute and priceless, such as privacy, liberty, health care, education, the "right" to vote, and others. While we may all agree that each of these attributes of life is a very important contributor to human happiness, all of them involve costs and these costs should be weighed against the benefits these attributes provide. While Patrick Henry may have once said, "Give me liberty or give me death," most people would accept less than perfect liberty, privacy, or voting privileges to stay alive and less than perfect health care and education to have more and higher-quality goods and services.

Tradeoffs are inevitable. This fact makes the implementation of absolute "rights" infeasible and undesirable. The U.S. Bill of Rights may serve as good "rule of thumb" policy. It has no doubt achieved far more good than harm overall. Nevertheless, this revered Bill does not constitute best public policy. At some point, the costs of obtaining more of any "right" will inevitably exceed the benefits.

There is no law that says laws must be written using best economics. But there should be!

48.   We Are Running Out of Natural Resources

Obviously, our planet is finite. Moreover, annual worldwide consumption of many of our world's natural resources (for example, crude oil) continues to increase. Doomsday predictions of an impending economic catastrophe have been voiced by many. But for all practical purposes, we will never completely run out of natural resources such as oil. Economics will ensure this.

When a natural resource such as oil becomes scarce, our economy's price system goes to work. Scarcity drives up prices. Higher prices provide *incentives* for people to (1) conserve the resource, (2) substitute other less scarce resources, and (3) look harder to find more of the resource. So, for example, if oil becomes scarcer, its price and the price of gasoline (which is refined from crude oil) will rise, prompting drivers to purchase more fuel efficient cars and drive less, car manufacturers to develop new hybrid or electric cars, and oil companies to look harder and dig deeper to find new oil reserves.

The final drop of oil will never be extracted from the earth. The last drop would be far too expensive to extract, more costly than alternative energy sources available today. Moreover, by the time we got to that last drop, new technologies would no doubt exist that would greatly reduce or eliminate our demand for oil (fuel cell cars?).

Thus, the problem is not that we are likely to ever run completely out of natural resources such as oil. Indeed, the world seems further away from running out of oil today than in the past. For example, in 1970, known world crude oil reserves were roughly 500 billion barrels, while world annual consumption was approximately 17 billion barrels. With these reserves and this rate of consumption, we should have already run out of oil! Moreover, annual world oil consumption had risen to more than 28 billion barrels by the turn of the century. Yet we still have oil, more oil in fact. Known oil reserves today are over 1 trillion barrels, thanks to new exploration and new exploration technologies.

A real problem consumers may face in the future is that the prices of certain natural resources may rise substantially if demand for these resources increase and if these resources become scarcer. But this day may be a long way off. *Real* prices for natural resources have generally fallen or stayed constant over the last century. Many new discoveries and new technologies that have reduced production costs have increased the *supply* of most natural resources dramatically. These supply increases have at least kept pace with the growing *demand* for natural resources, keeping prices from rising. For example, the real price of copper is approximately the same as it was 125 years ago, despite the fact that annual consumption is about 100 times greater today! There is no compelling evidence that this trend will not continue, at least into the near future.

So, don't worry about doomsday, at least not because of simplistic claims that we are going to run out of natural resources any time soon.

49.   Recycling Paper Saves Trees

Trees are wonderful, and sometimes recycling makes economic sense. But if you want more trees in the world, you might think twice about recycling your paper.

Suppose 100% of every piece of paper and every wood product was recycled. Assuming the *demand* for paper and other wood products stays constant, there would be no need to cut down another tree. But what financial *incentive* would landowners have to plant trees and protect their existing trees? Without a demand for new wood products, there would be no reason to *supply* wood to the market. Ultimately, the number of trees would likely fall, not rise. (Similarly, if we all became strict vegetarians, the population of cows would fall). Thus, counter-intuitive as it seems, if you want more trees around, you may want to use more paper and throw more paper away.

50.   Oil Companies Gouge Consumers at the Pump

Almost every time gasoline prices spike upward a chorus of criticism can be heard from politicians, the media, and the general public about how U.S. oil companies are ripping off consumers again. But if oil price increases always lead to higher profits for oil companies, and if these higher prices are simply the result of oil executives deciding to raise prices any time they want, why wouldn't U.S. oil executives have raised prices earlier and kept them high? Why wouldn't they raise prices still higher today?

The answer is that U.S. oil executives can't increase profits any time they want by simply raising prices. For example, any single company that decided to raise gas prices would lose sales to their competitors. If all companies somehow were able to collude and jointly agree to restrict sales and raise gas prices, their executives would risk being thrown in jail for *price fixing*.

Prices of goods in a market economy, including the prices of oil and gas, are determined by the forces of *supply* and *demand*. The price of crude oil, and the price of gasoline made from crude oil, rises when supply falls or demand rises. For example, in the spring of 2004 gasoline prices rose sharply in the United States due largely to unrest in the Middle East and OPEC (Organization of Petroleum Exporting Countries) supply caps which limited oil supply, combined with increased demand for oil in the United States and China.

But if gasoline price hikes are not the result of oil executive impulses, why are U.S. gasoline prices so volatile compared with other market prices, such as car prices? The reasons why U.S. gasoline prices fluctuate are that crude oil supplies are frequently interrupted by supply shocks (such as strikes in Venezuela, Wars in the Middle East, new OPEC production agreements, etc.) and because the *elasticity of demand* for gasoline is *inelastic*. For example, when the cost of importing crude oil into the United States rises because of a sudden supply shock, most of this higher cost can be passed on to consumers almost immediately in the form of higher gasoline prices. Since good substitutes for buying gasoline do not exist for most consumers, they will continue buying gas at these higher prices. Thus, gas prices can rise suddenly, or fall suddenly after oil supplies increase again.

It is, therefore, shifts in supply and demand that cause gasoline prices to increase, not sudden decisions by U.S. oil company executives to make more profits by raising prices. It may be fair, however, to partially blame the OPEC cartel for fixing crude oil prices at high levels at the expense of world oil consumers. Unfortunately, U.S. law cannot ensure competition among foreign suppliers.

51.   Stock Brokers Can Help You Pick Winner Stocks

Common sense suggests that stockbrokers and stock analysts have expertise that can help investors select the best stocks to buy. But sometimes common sense is wrong. Economic theory strongly indicates that individual stock prices follow a "random walk" and generally are not predictable. This theory has been extensively tested with real world data. Unless stockbrokers are privy to inside information (which is illegal to share or use), they can't predict stock prices any better than you can (see Lesson 11).

Stock market professionals can offer valuable services to their customers. But the myth that these professionals are most able to predict the direction of individual stock prices is very widespread and very much in need of debunking. Many thousands of people spend their valuable time and money every day listening to and following the advice of so-called stock "experts" who often offer worthless advice regarding which stocks to buy and sell.

Unfortunately, it is difficult to convince investors and students of the counter-intuitive finding that picking stocks is a random game, possibly because of the somewhat complex economic arguments involved regarding the "efficient market theory" of stock prices. These arguments fill the economic literature but are little understood elsewhere. Plus, most everyone has heard of people who have struck it rich in the stock market, even during down market years. It may seem these people must have special knowledge or skills. Economic theory and evidence, however, strongly indicates that the real reason why some people win big in the stock market is luck (or perhaps, inside information). But very few people read economic journals.

Fortunately, common sense isn't always wrong. It is common sense (not an economic journal) that tells us that if stockbrokers really knew which stock prices would increase, they would buy the winner stocks themselves rather than tell you to buy them. Yet there is no shortage of brokers who are willing to advise you (in return for a fee) which stocks to buy.

52.   Criminals Are Irrational

It is a common belief that most, if not all, criminals are irrational. But this belief is surely wrong. Even entirely self-satisfying criminals consider the consequences of their actions and respond rationally to *incentives*. Before committing a crime, most criminals will consider and weigh factors such as the potential payoff from the crime, the likelihood of being caught, and the penalty if they are caught. For example, if the probability of being caught of stealing $1,000 equaled one, and the penalty of being caught stealing $1,000 exceeded $1,000, surely few criminals would attempt such a theft. Alternatively, if the probability of being caught and the penalty if caught is low, then stealing will be "profitable" and more theft would be expected. Thieves may be immoral, but this does not mean they are irrational.

Even murderers are, at least to some degree, rational. If murderers were completely irrational, then they would not consider the consequences of their actions at all. Thus, the likelihood of someone committing murder would not depend on whether murders were punished or not. Do you think a potential murderer would be more likely to commit murder if murder was legal and not penalized in any way? If you do (I do!), then you understand that at least some murderers consider the consequences of their actions and are thus rational to some degree.

53.   The News Is "Fair and Balanced"

Deciding what to believe about what you read, hear, or see in the news is often challenging. Most news organizations are profit-maximizing businesses. As such, economics drives the type and quality of information you receive from them. As a consequence, the news you receive is all too often biased, of relatively little importance, inaccurate, or overly simplistic.

Be aware and beware of bias in the news. Since the news industry is in business to sell news, they may have an economic *incentive* to be biased. For example, news sellers know that sensational news sells. Thus, the news industry has an incentive to exaggerate the importance of news events. A news source may label every problem a crisis, every ill-advised deal a scandal, every bad weather day a life-threatening event, and every political race a cliff-hanger. The news media often dramatizes less than newsworthy stories for entertainment value. A dramatized story of a single celebrity's divorce may sell a lot more newspapers than news stories about how 43,000 Americans die each year in auto accidents or how over a million people die worldwide each year from preventable cases of malaria.

Some news sources have a political bias. Such bias may initiate from the political preferences of the executives leading these organizations. But more likely, such bias may arise as a consequence of profit-maximizing behavior. Consider the Fox News Network. Fox News has successfully marketed its product—conservatively slanted news reporting and commentary—to capture a large market niche: people who like viewing conservatively slanted news reporting and commentary. Most people prefer listening to news reports and commentary that confirm rather than challenge their beliefs (for example, few Republicans listen to Al Franken, and few Democrats listen to Rush Limbaugh). The psychological reason behind this observation is called "cognitive dissonance"—the theory that it is mentally unpleasant for people to receive information inconsistent with their personal views. So, by offering conservatively slanted news and commentary, Fox has been able to capture a large percentage of a large market—conservative, Republican viewers. Bias in the news can be the result of good business economics.

At times, economic considerations pressure news organizations to present less than complete or inaccurate information. News organizations have limited resources to investigate and verify stories. For example, a news reporter may have the time and resources to check but not double-check the credibility of a source. Moreover, competition pressures news organizations to be the first to release "breaking news" stories. Sometimes such pressure may compromise accuracy (such as when news sources projected Al Gore the "Winner" over George Bush). Of course, news organizations that are inaccurate too often may lose credibility and be penalized in the marketplace. But some degree of inaccuracy is an expected result of economic forces.

Finally, news reports tend to be overly simplistic. For example, economic stories may be overly simplified because a reporter or the reporter's market audience may not be sufficiently schooled in economics. Particularly with regard to complex economic news, overly simplistic reporting can lead readers to form entirely wrong conclusions.

To a large degree, you can protect yourself from biased, immaterial, inaccurate, and simplistic news reporting and commentary by educating yourself about subjects such as economics, American government, and basic science. For example, macroeconomics is always in the news. Without a good understanding of the basic language of macroeconomics (What does GDP, CPI, FOMC, etc., mean?), you will be unarmed in your battle to effectively comprehend and filter the news. But even well-educated readers can be fooled by bad news reporting and commentary. You also should protect yourself by considering the motives of the sources of your news and adjusting your interpretation of what you read, hear, and see accordingly. Always be skeptical, but avoid destructive cynicism. Despite economic pressures, some reporters and commentators still try their best to give you the straight scoop.

CHAPTER 4:
Solve Riddles and Mysteries:
Why the World Is as It Is

Introduction

This chapter invites you to look through the economic microscope to see what would otherwise go unseen. The questions below challenge you to become an "economic naturalist." Many of these questions do not look like economic questions, but you will see that they all are. Like the biologist who investigates the natural living world, or the astronomer who studies the natural world of the cosmos, you can use economics to study and understand the natural economic world that surrounds you. By thinking critically, asking "Why?" until reasons are found, looking beyond the obvious, and applying basic economic principles, you can solve many of the world's puzzles, riddles, and mysteries. The examples below are fascinating and fun to try to solve. More importantly, practicing using economics to solve these mysteries will provide you valuable training in critical thinking that will help you answer questions and solve problems throughout your life.

54. Why Are Americans Getting Heavier?

The mystery of expanding waist lines in the United States can be best understood by first identifying the determinants of weight gain and then examining how the *incentives* for people to gain weight have changed over time.

Essentially, someone's weight is determined by the number of calories they consume and the number of calories they burn. So, how have the costs and benefits of consuming calories changed over time?

In *real* terms, the dollar costs of purchasing most food products have been falling in the United States. This is due in large part to advances in agricultural technology that have greatly reduced the cost of producing most food products.

87

Moreover, the *opportunity cost* of consuming high-calorie "fast foods" compared with lower-calorie prepared meals has been falling, since prepared meals typically require more time and the opportunity cost of people's time has been rising (because Americans generally have greater employment and entertainment opportunities to occupy their time today). Finally, the widespread availability of microwave ovens also has lowered the time cost associated with consuming food.

Meanwhile, the benefits of consuming food have been rising. People eat for energy, but also for enjoyment. The vast variety and quantity of good-tasting food available to average Americans today has made eating more pleasurable than ever before. Thus, with costs lower (especially for fast foods) and benefits higher, people are eating more.

How have the costs and benefits of burning calories changed over time? Since, as discussed above, the opportunity cost of people's time has been increasing, the opportunity cost to people of spending their time exercising has been increasing. Meanwhile, the benefits associated with physical activity have been falling as employment opportunities have shifted from physical labor to office place positions and as labor saving technologies have invaded our homes (pushing computer keyboards and TV remote control buttons does little for our waistlines). Thus, people are moving their bodies less and burning fewer calories.

The bottom line—because of the way American's incentives associated with eating and moving their bodies has changed, they are consuming more and burning less calories. The result is weight gain.

55.   Why Is It Rational to Be Ignorant Sometimes?

It makes good sense to be and remain ignorant when the *opportunity costs* of obtaining knowledge about something outweigh the expected benefits of having the knowledge. Information is costly. It takes time, effort, and often money to be informed. Sometimes these costs exceed the expected benefits of the information. For example, it would be irrational for you to spend hours shopping for the best price to buy a candy bar. Thus, people typically make decisions based on incomplete information.

As a consequence, people sometimes make wrong decisions, decisions that end up not serving their interests. For example, suppose you buy a candy bar because it looks good, but then discover you dislike it and discard it after one bite. Your decision to buy the candy bar was rational. You simply based your decision on incomplete information (looks only). It would have been irrational for you to spend a lot of time, effort, and money surveying people to obtain their opinions about the candy bar and analyzing the ingredients in the candy bar so that you could have made a more informed decision. Thus, you acted on incomplete information and, in retrospect, made a mistake. But it was not a mistake to have acted on incomplete information. People make mistakes, even when they act wisely.

56.   Why Don't More People Vote?

During the amazingly close Bush-Gore U.S. presidential election of year 2000, only 51% of the voting age American population voted. Even during the fiercely contested Bush-Kerry 2004 presidential election, which resulted in record-breaking voter turnout totals, only about 60% of the voting age population voted. If people care about public policy, and if elected officials make public policy, then why don't more people vote? The answer is that for many people the costs of voting outweigh the expected benefits.

It is costly to register an informed vote. It takes significant time and effort *opportunity costs* to learn about public issues and the candidates' positions on these issues. Voting also incurs time and travel opportunity costs on Election Day.

Meanwhile, the expected benefits from voting to the average voter are typically quite small. While the results of the election may have a large cumulative impact on society, individual voters may perceive the impact on themselves to be small and very uncertain. Insufficient *incentives* may exist for individual voters to consider the *externality benefits* to society of registering an informed vote. Moreover, even when voters believe the results of an election will be important to them personally, they realize the chance that their one vote will change the result of the election is very, very, small. Finally, even if one vote would change an election result, there is always the significant possibility that the winning candidate will disappoint the voter after Election Day. Thus, it may be perfectly rational for some people to remain ignorant about politics and not participate in elections, even when the results of elections matter greatly.

Given this analysis of the costs and benefits of voting, maybe the more difficult and interesting question to ask is— "Why do so many people vote?" Perhaps the reason why many people do vote is that other benefits associated with participating in the political process exist. Some people enjoy following public issues and politics. They may be entertained by political "races." For these people, the costs of staying informed may be insignificant or negative and voting may be fun. Some people may get "psychic benefits" from voting. They may simple feel better about themselves for having performed their "civic duty." In any case, the decision to vote, like other decisions, rests on the relative costs and benefits involved.

57.   Why Is the Divorce Rate Greater for Celebrities?

Even though celebrities tend to be wealthy and have access to conveniences and luxuries that should ease the potential stresses of marriage, it is not surprising we so often hear about the break-up of celebrity marriages after very short periods of matrimony. While no definitive statistics exist regarding this matter, anecdotal evidence (such as testimony from celebrity divorce attorneys) suggests that the celebrity divorce rate may far exceed the divorce rate of the general population. Basic economics predicts this result. To understand this phenomenon, we need only apply the concept of *opportunity cost*.

First, the opportunity cost of a celebrity's time is very high. Superstar athletes, singers, and movie stars have many opportunities to make wealth and do exciting things. Everyone wants a piece of their time. For example, a famous movie star might be faced with the following choices regarding how to spend her time: (1) fly to New York to make a TV commercial and make a hundred thousand dollars, (2) fly to Hollywood and start a new multimillion dollar motion picture, or (3) stay home and spend time with her spouse. Consequently, since their opportunity cost of time is so high, celebrities may spend less time with their spouses and this may contribute to high celebrity divorce rates.

Perhaps more importantly, when celebrities choose to marry, they typically impose a high opportunity cost on themselves. When married (presuming fidelity), celebrities forego many "opportunities." Clearly, a relatively poor economics teacher will have many less opportunities for new partners after a break-up than would a rich and famous sports athlete. Since a celebrity's cost of being married is so high, we should expect celebrities to stay in "committed" relationships for relatively short periods of time. All people respond to *incentives*.

58.   Why Are Families Getting Smaller?

At the beginning of the 20th century, the average woman in the United States had more than three and three-quarter children. Today, the average woman in the United States has approximately two children. The cause of this dramatic transformation of the American family can be understood by examining how the costs and benefits of small versus large families have changed throughout the last century.

First, the *opportunity cost* of having children has risen substantially in the United States. For many decades, women worked primarily in the home. But in modern-day America, most women have joined the workforce and many have professional careers. At a minimum, having a child involves an interruption in a woman's career. Thus, the costs of having children today are significantly higher than in the past.

Second, the benefits associated with large families have fallen in the United States. Many years ago in the United States (and today in many less developed countries), children were very much needed to work on farms and care for their parents when they became elderly. While such needs still exist, they have declined in modern-day America because of the sharp decline in agricultural employment, rising standards of living, and public assistance programs for the elderly such as Social Security and Medicare.

Finally, the benefits associated with large families have fallen because of another reason—birth control. In the past, a significant benefit associated with having children was the enjoyment associated with creating them. Today, because of inexpensive and effective birth control methods, sexual relations can occur without significant risk of unwanted pregnancy. Thus, the benefits associated with making children have fallen.

Facing rising costs and falling benefits of having large families, Americans have chosen to have fewer children. People respond to *incentives*. However, the costs and benefits of having children haven't changed significantly in less developed countries of the world. Not surprisingly, birth rates remain very high within these impoverished countries.

59. Why Do White Men Make More Money than Women and Minorities?

In the year 2003, median income in the United States for white women was only 78%, and for black males only 76%, of the median income received by white males. Hispanic Americans fared even worse than white women and black Americans. Is discrimination the cause of these earnings differences? Are employer prejudices to blame?

Economists have not fully explained these wage differences, but economic analysis indicates that:

(1) *Employer* prejudice is unlikely to be a major source of earnings differentials,

(2) *Some* employer discrimination is rational (though perhaps still wrong from society's viewpoint),

(3) *Part* of the observed earnings differentials is not directly caused by employment discrimination, and

(4) Discrimination must be *widespread* for significant wage differentials among groups to persist.

When most people think of job discrimination, they think of a manager who pays lower wages or refuses to hire someone of a different race, sex, or age because of pure prejudice. While employer prejudice is certainly possible, economics argues that such prejudice is unlikely to remain a significant cause of earnings differentials. Employers who hire people based on factors other than expected productivity are punished by the marketplace. Their companies will lose out to other companies that are not prejudiced. Thus, competition provides powerful *incentives* for managers not to hire based on prejudice.

On the other hand, *consumer* prejudice is more likely to be the cause of wage differentials among certain groups of people. For example, if consumers don't trust women auto mechanics, no matter how competent they actually are, auto shop managers will want to hire and pay higher wages to male employees. In this case, the marketplace punishes employers who do *not* discriminate.

When consumer prejudice exists, it may be perfectly rational for employers to discriminate against certain groups. Employers also may rationally discriminate against individuals within certain groups because of statistical probabilities associated with the individual's group. For example, employers may prefer to hire men rather than women because women are more likely to quit their jobs to raise children. While such employer discrimination may be judged unfair and wrong by society, it is nonetheless rational and consistent with profit-maximizing behavior.

Part of the observed earnings differentials is not the direct result of employment discrimination. For example, educational attainment is higher among whites than among minority groups. Thus, whites may be more productive employees and earn higher salaries because of this fact. But studies have estimated that productivity factors such as education, experience, job choice, and geographic location account for only a part of the earnings differences among white males, white women, and minorities. Moreover, it is important to recognize that differences in productive factors such as educational attainment may be caused by the unequal opportunities available to different groups in society. Indeed, earnings differentials may cause educational differentials, which may cause earnings differentials to persist.

Finally, for discrimination to cause persistent earnings differentials, it must be widespread and not limited to particular industries. For example, suppose employers in industry A discriminate against women, causing women to look for jobs in nondiscriminatory industry B. Wage rates in industry A would increase due to the reduced *supply* of labor and wage rates in industry B would fall due to the increased supply of labor. But then more men would look for jobs in higher paying industry A rather than industry B, driving wage rates in industry A back down and wage rates in industry B back up. In the end, men would work in industry A and women in industry B, but overall wages for men and women would be unchanged (assuming both industries paid equal wages to begin with). This may, at least in part, explain why some occupations (like auto mechanics) are dominated by men and other occupations (like kindergarten teachers) are dominated by women. In any case, employer prejudice in one or a few industries should not cause significant earnings differences among different groups. The fact that unexplained earnings differences appear to persist suggests that some discrimination may remain widespread.

60.   Why Does Democracy Sometimes Fail?

Democracy may be the best political system around, but it is definitely not fail-proof. Democracy does not always lead to policies that best serve the public interest.

One problem with majority-rule democracy is that it may not reflect intensity of want. For example, suppose 51% of the population slightly prefers no policy change, while 49% of the population intensely prefers a policy change. If everyone votes on the policy, the vote of "no" will prevail, even though a policy change would generate net benefits to society.

Now imagine a thousand such policy choices that had to be voted on one at a time. In each case, the "no" votes would prevail and no policy changes would occur. But, if for each of these policy choices the minority's preferences are much more intense than the majority's preferences, it is entirely possible that *everyone* would be made better off if all of these policy changes were enacted, since each person would likely be a minority voter on some issues. If the thousand policies were lumped together for a single vote, it is entirely possible that everyone would vote yes, even though each policy voted on separately would not pass.

Almost the reverse of the tyranny of majority problem described above is another potential failure of democratic government—the special influence of special interest groups.

61. Why Do "Special Interests" Prevail Even When Almost Everyone Loses?

Some public policies generate large benefits to a small number of people (such as a specific industry) and impose small costs on a large number of people (such as consumers or taxpayers). Often politicians have *incentives* to support such policies, even when the total costs of such policies outweigh the total benefits.

Consider the sugar industry. The U.S. sugar industry benefits from government policies that restrict the importation of sugar from foreign countries into the United States. But consumers pay for trade barriers such as *quotas* and *tariffs* through higher product prices. The cost on U.S. consumers of sugar trade barriers has been estimated to equal nearly $2 billion annually, which undoubtedly far exceeds the benefits to those in the sugar industry. Nonetheless, politicians continue to support this *protectionist* trade policy. Why?

The $2 billion cost to consumers is spread out across the entire population. Per person, the cost is only $6 or $7 per year. For such a small cost, it is probably not worth it for individuals to pay attention to this issue and certainly not worth it to attempt to do anything about the issue. That is, the cost of action exceeds the benefit of action for any individual consumer. Rational ignorance prevails, and few actively oppose the policy.

Politicians have little incentive to oppose these trade barriers either, since those harmed by the policy are largely uninformed and uninterested.

Meanwhile, even though the benefits to the sugar industry of these trade barriers may be far less than $2 billion per year, these benefits accrue to a relatively small number of people. It is worth it to the sugar industry interest group members to research all of the issues, lobby congress, contribute campaign funds to politicians who will support the barriers, etc. Politicians thus have a strong incentive to support these harmful trade barriers.

Unfortunately, additional examples of special interests prevailing over the public interest are not at all hard to find.

62.   Why Have Socialist Economies Virtually Disappeared?

Socialism collapsed around the world largely because it proved to be a very poor economic system. Consistently low living standards provided the evidence and the discontent to induce most socialist countries to reform their economies. A few decades ago nearly half the world's population lived in socialist countries. Today only a few countries, like poor Cuba and very, very poor North Korea, maintain a centrally planned socialist economic system. Meanwhile, long time socialist countries such as China, the countries formerly part of the Soviet Union, and the countries of Eastern Europe have been transforming their economies away from central planning and toward free market capitalism. While this transition to freer markets has been difficult, economic progress has resulted. China's conversion, for example, has produced the second largest and one of the fastest growing economies in the world.

But why didn't socialism work? The key principles of socialism—government (as opposed to private) ownership of property and control of pricing, production, and distribution decisions, seem workable and "fair." But socialism failed for at least two major reasons.

First, government planning agencies were incapable of knowing how to coordinate the millions of economic activities involved in running an economy. Even basic decisions, such as choosing the optimal number of pencils to produce and deciding how to produce them, can be quite complex requiring information that is dispersed among millions of consumers and workers. In a market-based price system, prices automatically adjust to convey information about what goods people want and which production methods are least costly. But in a socialist economy, pricing, production, and distribution decisions were left to government agency guesswork. Not surprisingly, such guesswork led to regular shortages, the routine production of poor quality goods, and an overall low standard of living for the people living in socialist countries.

Second, and perhaps most importantly, socialist economies did not provide individuals with sufficient *incentives* to work hard, innovate, and invest in their own productivity. Under socialism, all property is owned by the government. Individuals in socialist countries did not own the rights to earnings from their work or innovations. Thus, it too often was not in workers' self-interest to work hard, develop new products and inventions, and find innovative ways to reduce production costs. Generally, workers were distributed the same rewards regardless of their individual productivities. As a result, productivity was low, fewer high-quality goods were produced, and standards of living suffered. More equality may have been achieved through socialism, but equality is no great accomplishment if everyone is poor.

All of this is not to say that some role for government intervention in economies is not merited. In fact, no country's economy in the world today is entirely capitalist. All nations employ a "mixed" economic system, typically where most economic decisions are made through markets, but some are made by government agencies. Sweden, for example, has maintained a relatively high standard of living for its citizens while combining free market principles with active government planning. But full-blown socialism has proven to be a dismal failure.

Let's hope the people of the remaining socialist countries can overcome their defiant political leaders and reform their failed economies.

63.   Why Did the Price of a Newspaper Rise by 2 Billion Percent in Two Years?

When fueled by bad government policy, inflation can spiral way out of control. An extreme example of this occurred in Germany after World War I. By 1924, the prices of products in Germany were more than 100,000,000,000,000 times greater than they were just 10 years before! During the two-year peak period of Germany's bout with *hyperinflation*, the price of a newspaper rose from 1/3 mark to 70 million marks. Incredibly, money became more valuable as wallpaper or firewood than for what it could buy. Destructive bouts of hyperinflation have plagued modern day economies too. Particularly bad hyperinflations occurred in several South American and Eastern European countries throughout the 1980s and 1990s. Perhaps the worst modern day hyperinflation occurred in Nicaragua: Between June 1986 and March 1991, prices went up nearly 12 billion percent!

Hyperinflations are caused when governments issue far too much money. When governments want to spend, they have three options for obtaining money: collect taxes, borrow, or create new money. Countries in economic distress caused by war, bad policy, or other events may need to spend money to pay off large debts. But for such countries, raising money through taxation or borrowing may not be feasible. The third option, however, is always feasible and relatively painless, in the very near term. But when too much money is distributed, more money chases the same goods and services and inevitably prices rise. Sometimes, as we have learned through history, prices rise and rise and rise.

64. Why Are You Better Off than the Richest Person Who Ever Lived?

Suppose you have all the money in the world, but you lived 100 years ago. Would you be happier than you are now?

Despite your money, you wouldn't be able to buy many of the things you are accustomed to having today. You couldn't use your money to telephone a friend, use a computer, travel in an airplane, drive in a reliable car, turn on an air conditioner during a steamy day, watch a television show, etc. You also wouldn't be able to buy pain alleviating and potentially lifesaving medicines and medical treatments that are commonplace today. Modern day antibiotics, painkillers, surgical procedures, etc. would be nowhere to be found. Many of your friends and family would die young (average life expectancy was less than 50 years old).

One hundred years ago, John D. Rockefeller was a 65-year-old extraordinarily rich man. Rockefeller had been President of the Standard Oil Company. By aggressively expanding his company throughout the late 19th century, Standard Oil became a virtual *monopoly*. Standard Oil's market dominance allowed it to capture *economies of scale* that lowered *average costs* and to use monopoly power to charge high prices. The result was enormous profit for Standard Oil and for Rockefeller. Rockefeller's wealth approached nearly $1 billion in 100-year-ago dollars. Adjusting for inflation to convert this figure into *real* present-day dollars, Rockefeller's wealth would equal roughly $200 billion dollars, ranking him a few times as wealthy as the wealthiest American living today (Bill Gates). Indeed, Heritage Magazine ranked Rockefeller as the richest American who ever lived. But was Rockefeller better off than you are today? Technological progress is a wonderful thing.

65. Why Are Buffalos Nearly Extinct and Cows So Plentiful?

Buffalos, elephants, rhinoceros, and many other valuable wildlife species have been or are being threatened with extinction primarily because they are killed by humans. But humans kill many more cows than they kill buffalos, elephants, and rhinos combined. Why then is there no shortage of cows?

The reason cows and other farm animals such as chickens and pigs are so plentiful is that they are privately, not commonly, owned. Wildlife roams freely. Wild animals are owned by everyone, not any one. Poachers kill valuable species as quickly as they can because if they delay, someone else may beat them to it. This is the so-called *Tragedy of the Commons.*" When valuable resources such as animals are *common property*, there is little *incentive* for individuals to conserve these resources. Indeed, the end result for some species of wildlife can be extinction.

But cows and other farm animals are fenced in and legally assigned as *private property*. No one but the owner has the legal right to kill them. Farmers have an incentive to raise and conserve their animals, since they are legally protected against the threat of other people taking and killing them.

As with many of society's problems, the problem of endangered species is largely a problem about incentives and very much a problem involving economics.

66.   Why Are Diamonds More Expensive than Water?

Isn't water much more valuable than diamonds? Water is necessary for life. Diamonds are not essential for life. Thus, the total value people receive from water far exceeds the total value they receive from diamonds. So, water is more valuable than diamonds. But why then is water so cheap and are diamonds so expensive?

Since water is much more plentiful than diamonds, the additional or *marginal* value people receive from obtaining one more unit of water is far less than the additional or *marginal* value they receive from obtaining one more unit of diamond. Thus, people are willing to pay more for a diamond ring than for another gallon of water.

In the absence of government regulation, the prices of commodities such as water and diamonds are determined by the forces of *supply* and *demand*. Diamonds are much more expensive than water because the supply of diamonds is very low relative to the supply of water. If one day clean drinking water becomes very, very scarce, its price could rise far above that of diamonds.

67. Why Do Giants Whose Job Is to Put a Ball in a Hoop Make So Much Money?

It seems odd that someone whose job is to play basketball earns two hundred times more income than your favorite economics teacher and thirty times more income than the president of the United States. But in the private sector, the forces of *supply* and *demand* determine the price of labor (worker salaries) as well as the prices of goods and services. Superstar athletes make so much money because the supply of superstars is so low and the demand for them is so high. There is only one Shaquille O'Neal. There are tens of thousands of people willing to pay good money to see him play basketball. Shaq's team owner is making a smart business decision by paying him millions of dollars each year to put a ball through a hoop. Good teachers provide a valuable service to their students, but the supply of qualified teachers is relatively plentiful. Thus, unfortunately, there is no need for schools to offer multimillion-dollar salaries to fill teaching positions.

68. Why Should the World's Best Furniture Mover Never Move Furniture?

Just because someone is the best at doing a job doesn't mean they are the best person to do the job. Consider, for example, our seven-foot two-inch 300-plus-pound friend Shaquille O'Neal again. Suppose Shaq gets traded and decides to move his household belongings. There may be no one in the world more able to move furniture as quickly and easily as powerful Shaq. So, should he move his own furniture? Answer: Absolutely not!

The economic principle of *comparative advantage* states that a task should be done by whoever has the lowest *opportunity cost* of completing the task. Even though Shaq could move his furniture more quickly than a typical 150-pound mover, he should pay a mover to move his furniture because Shaq's opportunity cost of time is so high. If Shaq spent his time moving furniture, he would forego great opportunities, such as playing basketball in front of thousands of fans, doing commercials that would earn many thousands of dollars, or taking a luxurious vacation to anywhere he wishes. Shaq has comparative advantage in playing basketball and doing commercials; the mover has comparative advantage in moving furniture. Each should specialize in performing those tasks for which they have comparative advantage.

69. Why Should Farmers Hate Years When the Weather Is Great for Farming?

Good weather increases crop yields. If farmer X's crop yields increase while all other farmers' yields stay the same, then farmer X will be better off. But if good weather increases crop yields on all farms, all farmers may be worse off. Two reasons underlie this paradox.

First, good weather that increases crop yields results in an increase in the *supply* of food products. Greater supply means farmers must lower their prices in order to sell all of their products. Lower prices mean lower profits, unless farmers can sell a lot more of their products.

Second, the demand for food products tends to be *inelastic*. People buy nearly the same amount of food regardless of price. Thus, after good weather increases supply and causes farmers to lower prices, consumers won't buy significantly more food. The percentage fall in food prices will no doubt be larger than the percentage increase in food quantities sold. Thus, total revenues (prices times quantities sold) to farmers will fall.

This example illustrates what economists call the *fallacy of composition*. This fallacy occurs when a decision that makes sense from each individual's perspective within a group (such as each farmer deciding to sell more food) is detrimental to the group as a whole (all farmers receive lower prices). As another example of this fallacy, to see better you may decide to stand up at a rock concert. You may be better off standing. But what if everyone thinks like you and stands too? Then nearly every-one may have trouble seeing and be less comfortable. Thus, decisions that make sense for each individual may lead to all individuals being worse off.

70.   Why Does the Government Pay Farmers *Not* to Grow Crops?

For many years, the U.S. government has paid farmers of cer-tain crops to limit the acreage they cultivate. The primary pur-pose of these programs has been to artificially support the prices farmers receive for their crop. By providing an incentive (a bribe) to farmers to reduce the acreage they farm, *supply* is limited. When supply falls, prices and farmer revenues rise. This is particularly so because (as discussed in Lesson 69) the demand for many food products is relatively inelastic, meaning that nearly the same amount of food will be purchased regard-less of price. Higher prices could attract more people to be-come farmers, forcing prices down again. But since the supply of agricultural land is relatively fixed, these programs probably succeed in raising farmer incomes both through the bribes and higher crop prices. Why does the U.S. government wish to sub-sidize certain farmers, but not other farmers, fishermen, store-keepers, and most other business owners? The answer has to do with politics. To learn more, turn to Lesson 88.

71.   Why Would People Be Worse Off If They Were Given a Million Dollars?

Would you be better off if the government gave you a million dollars? Yes, you no doubt would. But if the government gave everyone a million dollars, everyone would no doubt end up worse off. As discussed in Lesson 39, money is of no value in and of itself. If the government handed you a million dollars but no new goods or services are created, a bit of inflation would be result (more money with the same goods must cause prices to increase). So, while you would be much better off with a million dollars and slightly higher prices, everyone else would be a little worse off because of the higher prices. The million dollars you received would not make the world richer; it would only make you richer relative to others.

But if everyone were given a million dollars from the government, this would ultimately result in nothing but inflation. No one's *real* wealth or purchasing power would change, because the same goods and services that existed before the handout would exist after the handout. Moreover, people would have to deal with costs associated with inflation, such as the *menu costs* to businesses of having to change all of their prices and other inflation related costs. Thus, we would all end up worse off from the government handout.

As explained in Lesson 100, there are times when an injection of money into the economy can temporarily induce people to produce more goods and services. Increasing the money supply (expansionary *monetary policy*) can be used to counteract an economy-wide *recession*. But in the long run, the only result of distributing more money is inflation.

72.   Why May People Lower Their Savings If They All Try to Save More?

Suppose for some reason, you decide to hold on to more cash. Perhaps you think the economy is shaky, investment opportunities are risky, and you could lose your job. So you decide to save a greater percentage of your income. Your savings will increase. But what if everyone thought and acted just like you? If everyone reduces their spending, business revenues and worker incomes will fall. So while each person may save a higher percentage of their income, their incomes may fall so much that everyone's total savings falls. This is the so-called "paradox of thrift" articulated by the famous macroeconomist John Maynard Keynes. According to *Keynsian* economists, the paradox of thrift could lead economies into *recession*.

In the long run, the paradox of thrift should not occur. As *Classical* school economists explain, businesses will continue lowering prices until they can sell their goods and services again. The workings of the price system should pull itself out of recession. But prices take time to adjust, especially in a downward direction. As Keynes famously observed, "In the long run we are all dead." In the meantime, attempts by people to save a higher fraction of their income could be counter-productive.

73. Why Do Airlines Care If You Stay Over a Saturday Night?

Have you ever wondered why airline tickets are often much cheaper if you stay over a Saturday night at your destination? This seemingly odd but entirely rational airline pricing strategy is an example of what economists call *price discrimination*.

To increase profits, airlines wish to charge different prices to different customers. Indeed, all business would like to charge each of their consumers a different price—the highest price each consumer would be willing to pay for the product or service being sold. But businesses don't know how much each of their consumers would be willing to pay. They could ask each buyer. But, obviously, buyers would have no incentive to reveal the most they would pay. Airlines do the next best thing. Airlines estimate a customer's willingness to pay for a ticket based on knowledge about when the customer is traveling.

Airlines know that business travelers have, on average, a much greater willingness and ability to pay high prices for tickets. Economists would say that business travelers' *elasticity of demand* is relatively *inelastic*. That is, businesses would buy nearly as many tickets if airlines raised prices. Airlines also know that vacationers are less willing to accept high ticket prices. Travel for vacationers is typically more optional and more difficult to afford than travel for business people. If airlines raise prices, vacationers may drive, take a train, or forego their trip entirely. Thus, economists say that vacation travelers' elasticity of demand is relatively *elastic*.

Airlines know they can increase their revenues by charging relatively high prices to business travelers (since most of them will buy tickets anyway) and relatively low prices to vacationers (since airlines gain a lot of sales by keeping prices for vacationers low). Who flies primarily during the week and returns before the weekend? Answer: Business travelers. Who flies primarily over weekends? Answer: Vacationers. Now you know why staying over a Saturday night can save you money.

74. Why Do Students Get Discounts for Movie Tickets but Not for Popcorn?

The reason why students often get discounts at movie theaters, museums, sporting events, etc., is the same reason why weekend airline travelers get discounts—businesses can increase profits if they can successfully *price discriminate*. On average, students' demand for tickets is more *elastic* than it is for most other ticket buyers. Students typically have less money and more free time. If a ticket price is too high, they may not buy a ticket or they might drive farther away to obtain a lower price from another business. By giving students discounts, theater owners can sell lots of tickets to students while maintaining higher prices for other customers who are less responsive to high prices.

But popcorn, candy, and other refreshments at the movie theater are different in an important way. Suppose theater owners gave discounts to students on all refreshments. Students attending the movies with their families would undoubtedly buy all of the refreshments for their families. We could even imagine some enterprising students buying refreshments and (quietly) reselling them to others in the audience who don't qualify for the discounts. Price discrimination does not work when the product being sold can be resold. Entrance into a theater, museum, or a sports event, (or a college!), cannot be resold and, thus, are prime candidates for price discrimination. But for goods that can be resold, those who qualify for discounts could buy extra, sell to others at a profit, and eliminate the original seller's opportunity to sell their product at an undiscounted, high price.

75.   Why Are There Too Many Lawyers?

Suppose you have been sued by someone. Suppose each of you has an equally good case (a 50% chance of winning). You must decide whether to hire a lawyer. Lawyers are expensive. If your opponent hires a lawyer and you don't, you will probably lose. If your opponent does not hire a lawyer and you do, you will probably win. Either way, you calculate it is in your interest to hire a lawyer. But your opponent will reason the same way and conclude that he or she will have to hire a lawyer too. Assuming that you both hire equally good lawyers, the chances of each of you winning given that both of you hire lawyers is 50%, the same as it is if neither of you hire lawyers. So, both of you would be better off not hiring a lawyer, saving the significant expense, and letting the judge decide. But both of you will hire a lawyer because, as already concluded, it is in both person's individual interest to do so!

This is an example of what economists call the *prisoner's dilemma*. Unless both parties can establish an agreement and insure that the agreement is not broken, both parties acting in their own self interest will end up making a decision that is undesirable for both parties considered jointly. There are many examples of this phenomenon in the world. The prisoner's dilemma has lead to arms races between nations, negative campaigns between politicians, and costly advertising and price wars between rival companies. It is not always true that individuals, acting in their self-interest, do what is best for society as a whole.

76.   Why Did the Tobacco Industry Support a Ban on Cigarette Advertising?

The tobacco industry was a strong supporter of the law that banned cigarette advertising on television. Why would any industry lobby for a law that restricted their marketing options? Answer: To avoid the prisoner's dilemma problem.

During the 1970s, the major cigarette companies spent lots of money attacking and counterattacking each other through television advertising. It was in each individual company's self-interest to continue advertising, since they would otherwise lose sales to their competitors who were advertising. But the high costs of advertising were hurting the industry overall. Thus, by getting the government to pass a law that banned cigarette advertising on television, the tobacco industry was able to solve their prisoner's dilemma problem and save a lot of advertising costs.

77.   Why Might Seat Belts Kill People?

Seat belts, air bags, and other safety features protect drivers from physical harm in the event of accident. Generally, they work. However, they also change the *incentives* facing drivers.

For example, by fastening their seat belts, drivers reduce the expected cost of driving recklessly and having an accident (since by fastening they reduce the risk that an accident will cause them physical harm). The benefits of driving recklessly (such as, saving time by driving very fast, talking on a cell phone, eating fast food, etc.) do not change after fastening a seat belt. If the costs of a behavior fall while the benefits remain the same, more of the behavior should be expected. That is, the protection provided by seat belts is likely to induce drivers to drive more recklessly. (If you don't believe this, consider the opposite. Suppose you didn't have a seat belt fastened and a sharp knife pointed from the steering wheel toward your heart as you drove. How fast would you drive?)

Thus, while the number of deaths per accident will fall because of seat belt use, if seat belts cause people to drive more recklessly, more accidents will occur. The net impact on traffic fatalities is unclear. In 1975, Sam Peltzman (from the well-respected University of Chicago) published a study in 1975 (in the well-respected *Journal of Political Economy*) that estimated that these opposite impacts were roughly the same size and that the net effect of seat belts on driver fatalities is approximately zero. This one study may not be enough to convince you that seat belts cause as many deaths as they prevent (it does not fully convince me). But when the expected increase in pedestrian deaths from increased accidents is factored in, it is entirely possible that seat belts kill more people than they save.

78.   Why Might Airline Safety Regulations Increase Accident Fatalities?

After the tragic events of 9/11/01, it seems only reasonable for the U.S. government to impose additional airline safety requirements. Such requirements may be necessary to reduce the risk that another such event could occur. But airline safety comes at a cost.

Increased security costs imposed on airlines reduce *supply* and drive up ticket prices. Higher ticket prices provide an *incentive* for people to *substitute* long distance driving for flying. Since driving (measured in terms of fatalities per mile traveled) is roughly 15 times as risky as flying on a scheduled commercial plane, costly airline safety requirements might cause more deaths than they save. To illustrate, it was estimated that roughly 350 more people died from auto traffic accidents than would otherwise have been expected to die during the three months following the events of 9/11/01. This number of fatalities exceeds the number of people killed on the downed flights that horrible day. Indeed, anything that discourages people from flying may indirectly cause an increase in auto accidents and cost lives. It is, therefore, vital that the unintended consequences of costly airline safety requirements be recognized and considered when assessing the desirability of such requirements.

79.   Why Might Pesticides Be Good for Your Health?

As a long-time employee of the U.S. Environmental Protection Agency, I understand that many pesticides can be harmful to human health. But pesticides can also be good for human health. Pesticides can increase crop yields. Increased crop yields increase *supply* and result in lower food prices. Lower prices lead to greater consumption. Greater consumption of "healthy foods" leads to improved human heath. For example, pesticide used on fruits and vegetables may cause some cancer risk. But it also may lead to significantly lower prices and greater consumption of fruits and vegetables. This increased consumption of fruits and vegetables may result in an overall reduction in cancer risks to consumers.

Another example of a harmful pesticide that could be used to improve human health is DDT. The United States banned the production and distribution of this harmful chemical in 1972 after it was observed that spraying caused damage to wildlife. However, DDT can be used to fight the terrible spread of malaria in many of the world's less developed countries by repelling mosquitoes carrying the malarial parasite. Malaria kills approximately 3,000 people a day in Africa alone. (That's more fatalities than those that occurred in New York by the horrific event on 9/11/01—and it is happening every single day!) Nevertheless, the United States does not support the distribution of DDT to these suffering countries. By making it difficult for poor countries to obtain DDT, the United States is most likely causing more health problems than it is preventing.

80.   Why Don't Laws that Mandate Benefits for Workers Benefit Workers?

Would you vote for a law that required your employer to provide you with "free" benefits such as health insurance, vacation time, and sick leave? Sounds good, but perhaps you should vote no.

Consider a law that required employers to provide their employees health insurance. Employees would receive a valuable benefit from this law, but this benefit would come at a cost to employers. To compensate for this per worker cost increase, employers will (after any wage contracts expire) lower the wages they offer their employees. If the cost to the employers of providing the health insurance exceeds the value of the benefits the employees receive from the health insurance, wage rates may fall so much that employees (and employers) are made worse off because of the law.

But what if the cost to the employers of providing the health insurance is less than the value of the benefits the employees receive from the health insurance? In this case, employers may still lower wages, but not so much that employees are worse off. Thus, both employers and employees may be better off. However, if this were the case, there would be no need for a law since employers would already have sufficient incentive to provide health insurance for their employees. Hence, surprisingly, laws requiring employers to provide benefits to their workers are unlikely to benefit workers.

81.   Why Do Self-Interested Businesspeople Serve the Public Interest?

In 1776, Adam Smith, the founder of economics, wrote about how people pursuing their own self-interest typically end up serving the public interest better than when they directly try to serve the public interest (for example, through government). Smith described why, within a *capitalist* economic system, business people have *incentive* (profit) to produce the goods and services the public wants and to do so as efficiently as possible. Business people know what the public wants and how much they want because they receive signals from the price system. When a product becomes highly valued, its price will rise, and the incentive for businesses to produce the product will rise. Thus, business people, driven by self-interest, produce and sell what the public wants. The result is gain to everyone through mutually beneficial exchange.

But government bureaucrats, even when they are well meaning, know less about what goods and services people want, how much they want, and how to produce goods and services. Moreover, government bureaucrats and politicians do not always have sufficient incentive to make decisions that best serve the public interest (see, for example, Lessons 61 and 87). History has proven that Smith was right. Capitalist economies have created much higher standards of living than have "centrally planned" economies run by government bureaucrats.

Smith, however, was wise to use the word "typically" rather than "always" when he asserted that business people serve the public interest better than governments. Some business activity does not serve the public interest. In such cases, our free market system fails (see Lesson 86) and the case for corrective government action is often strong.

82. Why in a World with Billionaires Does Half the World Live on Less than $2 a Day?

The World Bank estimates that as of the turn of the century, roughly half of the world's six billion people lived on less than two dollars per day. Millions of people suffer and thousands die every day because of extreme poverty. Preventable diseases like AIDS, dehydration, and malaria are running rampant and killing innocent victims in less developed countries. "It is unacceptable that 3,000 African children die every day from a largely preventable and treatable disease." These are the thoughtful words of multibillionaire Bill Gates speaking about the poverty driven crisis of malaria in Africa.

How in our modern world with multi-billionaires, high technology, and a sophisticated global economy, can this global crisis persist? A full analysis of this question would be complex and beyond the scope of this book, but what is clear is that a root cause of the failure of so many countries to grow out of poverty is political.

For economies to prosper, individuals must have sufficient *incentive* to work hard, to invest in their own productivity, and to produce goods and services that can be used by others. *Capitalism* provides this incentive. But capitalism must be permitted to work. Governments must first kick-start capitalism by establishing a secure foundation from which capitalism can work its magic. Then governments must stand back and allow free markets to work, intervening only in exceptional cases.

Capitalism cannot work in countries where self-interested dictators, instability, war, and political corruption rule. Nor can it work where legal and criminal justice systems are dysfunctional or nonexistent. For example, people have little incentive to start businesses when (1) a new dictator may take their business away, (2) they must wait many months and pay heavy bribes to bureaucrats to get required business permits, (3) crime is rampant, (4) contracts can't be enforced, (5) their business will be severely regulated, and so on.

Unfortunately, many of our world's poor countries have suffered and still suffer from these political and legal failures. As a consequence, the power of free market economics to raise standards of living has not been freed in these countries and millions of people suffer and die needlessly.

83.   Why Did the Author of this Book Voluntarily Cut His Salary in Half?

It may seem odd that a rational economist like me would accept a job that cut my salary in half. Personal finance dictates that I should not have made a career change to teach economics several years ago. But good personal finance is not always good economics. Economics is a much broader subject than finance. Moreover, it is good economics, not good finance, which should guide decision making.

My choice to change careers was based on a comparison of benefits and costs. The major cost of my decision was my (significant) loss of income. But my new position still provides me with enough income to cover my basic needs. Income above this amount, while desirable, is not that important to me. For example, my first $50,000 provides me much happiness or *utility* since it allows me to buy various "necessities." Another $50,000, while desired, is not as important to me, since it would be used to buy things of less importance to me. Economists call this fact an example of the *principle of diminishing marginal utility of income.*

Meanwhile, I received large non-financial benefits from accepting my teaching position, such as more enjoyable work, more "free" time, and (in my judgment) more opportunities to make positive differences to the lives of others (something I value greatly). For me, these benefits exceeded my loss of income. Everyone's preferences differ. The point is that people should define benefits and costs broadly, not just in financial terms, when making decisions. Indeed, my decision to change careers was very good economics. I have never regretted it.

CHAPTER 5:
Evaluate Public Policies:
In Pursuit of a Happier World

Introduction

This chapter is about using economics to assess a wide range of public policy issues. Understanding the impact and evaluating the desirability of public policies is challenging. To succeed, you must discipline yourself to be objective and apply economic thinking. Otherwise, you will likely be fooled by your own emotions and personal biases, as well as by politicians and other self-interested policy advocates.

The policy analyses below do not provide all the answers. This chapter provides only an overview assessment of pressing public policy issues. Moreover, the final evaluation of most public policy questions typically requires subjective value judgments. But by reading this chapter, you will learn how to use economics to better understand the news and to assess and predict the impact of public policies. Often with this knowledge, preferred policies will become obvious to you. Only with this knowledge will you be prepared to offer intelligent opinions and votes regarding the important public policy issues affecting our world.

Unfortunately, understanding what policies lead to a better world is only half the battle. The second half of the battle is actually making these policies happen. This second battle is probably more difficult than the first. But you *can* make a difference if you want to. Be politically active, vote, share what you know with others, write your political representatives, volunteer work or funds for an advocacy group, pursue a policy career in government, etc. I challenge you to use what you learn to leave the world a better, happier place than you found it. I offer you lessons from economics to help you meet this challenge.

84. The Amazing Power of Free Markets: Don't Fix What Ain't Broke

Economists have shown that competitive markets, free from government regulation, typically result in the most socially *efficient* outcome. This means that government intervention in our market economy will usually result in a decrease in the overall net benefits (total benefits – total costs) to society (for exceptions to this rule, see Lesson 86). Indeed, generally, even a perfectly wise and entirely benevolent ruler could not improve upon the free market outcome regarding what goods are produced and how these goods are produced and distributed. This is a powerful finding.

Because businessmen and businesswomen within a *capitalist* economy have a strong *incentive* (profit) to produce the products and services the public most wants and to produce these goods as efficiently as possible, they try hard to do so. They generally succeed because they receive signals from the market in the form of prices. For example, when a product becomes highly *demanded*, its price will rise and businesses will have incentive to *supply* more of the product. Goods supplied will end up in the hands of those who most want (and who are most able to pay for) them. In the end, everyone gains through voluntary and mutually beneficial exchange. Remarkably, all this occurs almost "invisibly" without any government direction.

Nobel prize-winning economist Milton Friedman popularized a story about the production of an ordinary pencil to illustrate the amazing power of our free market system. No one knows how to make a pencil, he observed. The know-how and effort to obtain, distribute, and effectively combine the wood, graphite, glue, brass ferrule, rubber eraser, paint, and the machinery necessary to paint and imprint letters for a single pencil requires literally thousands of individuals who are located all around the world. Who coordinates all of these individuals and the tasks they perform? No one does. It all happens almost invisibly through our free market system. Thousands of people, most of whom do not know each other or their customers, voluntarily choose to perform their little part toward the production of pencils so that you and I can go to the store and buy one for a couple of pennies. All of these workers benefit from their efforts, and so do consumers like you and me.

85. Regulation: A Tale of Unintended Consequences

Government regulation of markets can take various forms. Examples include price controls, licensing requirements, taxes, subsidies, and restrictions on the terms of sales. While often well meaning, such regulations typically impede the *efficiency* of our price system and lead to unintended and undesirable consequences.

To illustrate how government regulations may lead to adverse consequences, consider the regulatory policy of rent control. Numerous local governments throughout the United States employ some form of control over the rent that landlords can charge their tenants. For example, if the market *equilibrium* price for a 2-bedroom apartment is $1,000/month, a local government may establish a law prohibiting landlords from charging rent more than $750/month in an effort to help low-income renters. The initial effect of such a law would be a simple transfer of $250/month from landlords to their renters. But soon landlords would adjust to the law by reducing the number of apartments they *supply*. They may stop building new apartment buildings, convert their existing buildings to condominiums, or abandon their apartments altogether. Thus, one unintended result would be a shortage of apartments, which would make it difficult or impossible for many low-income renters to find apartments. But various other unintended and adverse results also may occur. Because too many renters would be searching for too few available apartments, landlords may (1) allow their buildings to deteriorate since they may not be able to afford repairs or because enough people would rent the inexpensive apartments in any case, (2) increase security deposits or other fees to get around the rent control regulation, and (3) discriminate against apartment seekers they don't like since there would be many others willing to rent their apartments at the rent control price.

In the end, the losses to landlords and renters who can't find apartments (or who live in deteriorating apartments) would exceed the benefits to those renters who manage to hold a rent-controlled apartment (that is, rent control is an economically inefficient policy). While the goal of helping low-income individuals obtain housing may be laudable, there are better ways to achieve this goal (such as through direct income redistribution) than by controlling rents that create rental housing shortages and other problems. Ultimately, these problems may hurt many of the lower-income individuals rent control policy advocates intend to help. The example of rent control is illustrative of the unfortunate complications that almost inevitably result when the government tampers with our market system.

86.   Free Market Failures: The Strong Case for Limited Government Action

Unfortunately, there are specific circumstances under which unregulated market capitalism fails to serve society's best interest. When these circumstances exist, a strong case for government intervention can be made. Potential examples of market failure include (1) *externalities*, (2) *public goods*, (3) incomplete information, (4) insufficient competition, (5) slow working markets, and (6) undesirable wealth distribution. To develop a framework for assessing public policies and understanding the role of government in our economy, it is important to be able to identify and understand each of these potential causes of market failure.

An externality occurs whenever someone's or some business's activity impacts the well-being of a bystander. For example, if I attempt to learn how to play the drums from within my townhouse, I will impose an external cost (or negative externality) on my neighbors. Alternatively, if I plant a beautiful garden in front of my townhouse, I may create an external benefit (or positive externality) for my neighbors if they enjoy viewing the garden. The problem with externalities is that since the cost or benefit from an externality generating activity does not fully accrue to the person performing the activity, there is insufficient *incentive* for individuals to consider the external costs and benefits of their actions. Consequently, too many negative and too few positive externalities may occur.

The classic example of a negative externality is environmental pollution. Businesses that pollute the air or water impose costs on the rest of society. These profit-maximizing businesses have little incentive to consider the costs they bear on others. Thus, without government intervention, polluters may keep polluting even if their pollution leads to significant illness and death. In this circumstance, unregulated capitalism clearly fails to serve the public good and government intervention is warranted (see Lesson 92).

Another strong case for a role for government in our economy involves the provision of public goods. Once produced, public goods have two unique characteristics: (1) more than one person can enjoy them simultaneously, and (2) no one can be excluded from enjoying them. Examples include national defense, flood control, lighthouses, street lights, clean air, radio broadcasts, and disease control.

Businesses will not *supply* public goods (except when they can bundle a public good with something else they are selling, such as they do with radio broadcasts and commercials). Businesses generally can't make a profit selling public goods because they can't exclude people who don't pay for using these good. For example, the public benefits from a dam to reduce flooding may exceed the costs of building the dam. Nevertheless, no business will build the dam since if it is built, everyone in a town will be protected whether they pay for the dam or not. Thus, governments should provide public goods when the benefits exceed the costs to society from doing so.

A third type of market failure may occur when buyers or sellers have incomplete information about the benefits and costs they will receive from a transaction. For example, if your auto mechanic advises that you need expensive work on your car, unless you too are a skilled mechanic, how do you know whether your car really needs the work? Perhaps the mechanic is just drumming up business. Rather than spending the time and effort getting more opinions and reading consumer report reviews, you may purchase the repairs without needing them. In this case, the free market system will have failed you. In some cases, government intervention to protect consumers from their lack of knowledge may be desirable (such as with certain consumer protection and safety regulations). In other cases, government provision of information may be better policy.

Markets also may not best serve the public interest when insufficient competition exists. A monopolist, for example, will restrict sales of their product so as to keep their price high. The result is more profit for the monopolist, higher prices for consumers, and typically less overall benefits to society than would occur if the market were more competitive. There is a role for governments to limit monopoly formation and power (such as through the passage of antitrust laws and price regulation). This said, monopolies are not always detrimental to society (see Lesson 45).

Another potential source of market failure exists during times when markets are adjusting to changing conditions. Prices respond to scarcity and surplus, but not instantaneously. Serious macroeconomic problems, such as recessions, can occur when prices get "stuck." During these times active government policy may be necessary to kick-start an economy (see Lesson 100).

Finally, free markets result in a very unequal distribution of wealth that may not maximize the well-being of society. A strong theoretical case can be made that governments can increase overall happiness by redistributing wealth to some degree (see Lesson 95). In practice, however, government redistribution programs may result in adverse unintended consequences.

Thus economics provides a checklist for testing whether a government policy may be justified. Whenever a government policy is proposed, you should ask yourself, "What is the market failure being addressed by the policy?" If no market failures exist, government intervention with our free market system will likely do more harm than good. If a market failure does exist, then the potential to improve society's overall well-being though government policies and programs also will exist, though this potential may not be realized in practice (see Lesson 87).

Of course, without any government, markets would have difficulty forming and operating. For market systems to function properly, governments must first establish a safe and orderly playing field. They must maintain political stability and establish and enforce the rule of law. In particular, they must establish and enforce property rights (to provide incentives for individuals to acquire and maintain property) and contract law (to ensure that business commitments are honored). In many less developed countries, corrupt or incompetent governments have failed in these tasks. As a result, the awesome potential of free markets to raise standards of living within these countries has never been realized (see Lesson 82).

87. But Governments Can Fail Too: The Economics of Politics

Potentially, governments can serve the public interest by fixing the failures of free market capitalism identified in Lesson 86. But will they? Sometimes they may, but other times they may make matters worse. Lessons from *public choice* economics, or the economics of politics, explain why the actions of government decision makers do not always serve the public good.

The personal interests of politicians and bureaucrats do not always align with the public interest. There are many examples of this problem. Politicians may be more concerned with re-election than with the public good. They may pander to special interest groups (see Lessons 61 and 88), ignore the long-term impacts of their policies (since they will be long gone before problems arise), or attempt to deceive the public for political gain. Bureaucrats within government agencies may be too interested in promotions, job security, or minimizing work effort to most effectively serve the public good.

Moreover, because of a lack of competition, government organizations tend to be less efficient than private organizations. A business must be well managed or else it will soon be beat out by its competitors. But government agencies face no such competitive pressure. They may remain slow and wasteful without major repercussion.

During my experience as an economist within the federal government, I met many hard-working federal employees who are dedicated to serving the public good. I also witnessed the development and implementation of government regulations that I believe served the public good. But at times, I also witnessed unmotivated employees, wasteful spending, politically driven decision making, and the implementation of regulations I believe did more harm than good. You would be wise to be skeptical of proposed government programs and regulations. Just because governments have the potential to improve upon free market outcomes, that doesn't mean they actually will.

88. Agricultural Policy: Farm Subsidies and Corporate Welfare

Each year, the U.S. government spends billions of taxpayer dollars subsidizing farmers. These subsidies take various forms such as agricultural price supports that guarantee above *equilibrium* prices, import tariffs that boost domestic agricultural prices, and payments to farmers who reduce the acreage they farm (see Lesson 70). European governments also heavily subsidize their farmers. But why subsidize farmers? Is there an agricultural market failure that needs correcting?

Unfortunately, the reason for agricultural subsidies lies within politics, not economics. Economists argue that agricultural markets should remain largely unregulated and unsubsidized. In the absence of government intervention, agricultural markets are typically very competitive and efficient. That is, the products that people want will be produced and produced at least cost. So, why not leave agricultural markets alone?

Some people argue that farmers should be subsidized to prevent food supply shortages. This argument is not supported by theory or fact. In the event of a crop shortfall, prices would increase inducing demand to fall and more suppliers to enter the market. Real world evidence supports this principle. Have you noticed shortages of fruits, vegetables, chicken, and beef? These farm products are not subsidized in the United States. Moreover, crop shortages were not a problem before farm subsidy programs were initiated.

Some people argue that farmers should be subsidized to save the "family farm." This argument is very weak. The vast majority of farm subsidies go to large corporations and wealthy landowners (some of whom don't even live in the United States!). The fraction of agricultural production coming from small farms is very small and becoming smaller. Corporate farms have taken over, mainly because of the cost savings they can achieve through *economies of scale*. Moreover, low-income farmers often rent the land they farm. Crop subsidies ultimately push up land rents benefiting the landowners, not the tenant farmers. Besides all of these arguments, why should taxpayers subsidize small business farmers but not other small businesses such as fishermen, storekeepers, and plumbers?

Who loses from farm subsidies? Millions, perhaps billions of people do. Taxpayers lose since some of their earned income is transferred to farm industries, consumers lose since they pay for government-imposed agricultural price supports and protectionist tariffs on agricultural products in the form of higher food prices, and millions of people living in the less developed countries of the world lose since they can't profitably sell their agricultural products because U.S. and European subsidies depress world agricultural prices.

So why do these farm subsidy programs persist? They persist because certain farm industries are very good at organizing themselves and lobbying politicians. For farmers, free markets mean competition and competition means reduced profits. To protect themselves from competition, farmers have learned how to work the political system, such as by contributing substantial campaign funds to politicians in both political parties who vote for price supports and other forms of farmer subsidies. Meanwhile, the general public knows little about all of this. Since the cost to any single person from agricultural subsidies is relatively small, it's just not worth it for individuals to spend their time, effort, and money researching the issues and lobbying politicians (see Lesson 55). The result is that agricultural special interests win at the expense of the overall public good (see Lesson 61).

Farm subsidy programs are perhaps the most egregious example of corporate welfare. They subsidize primarily large corporations and penalize taxpayers, consumers, and farmers from some of the poorest nations in the world. All too often, politics overrules good economics and the overall public interest.

89.   Education Policy: Is It Time for a Revolution?

Many believe America's public schools are failing America's children. Comparisons of the achievement levels of high school seniors in the United States versus the achievement levels of high school seniors in other developed countries suggest that this belief has merit. Can anything be done to improve the quality of education appreciably in the United States?

Governments in the United States (primarily state and local) fund and run most educational institutions, especially at the K–12 level. But should they? Good economic arguments can be made for government support of education. Education may generate positive *externalities* for society. For example, as you become better educated, you may become a better-informed voter and better citizen, you may learn how to better care for your family, or you may develop ideas or new products some of the benefits from which may accrue to others in society. Without government support for your education, you may not have sufficient incentive to educate yourself to the degree that most benefits society overall. Of course, education could create negative externalities for society too. Without education, for example, society would not have to worry about technology driven problems such as weapons of mass destruction. But overall, education probably creates more positive than negative externalities for society. If so, then some level of public support makes good economic sense.

Public funding of education also may be justified on equity grounds. Many believe that everyone should be provided an equal opportunity to learn. In practice, however, education funding (and education quality) is far from equally distributed in the United States since wealthy state and local governments provide considerably more support per student than do poorer state and local governments.

Public support of higher education is more difficult to justify on equity grounds. Is it fair to transfer average taxpayer dollars to college students whose future incomes are likely to significantly exceed the average worker's income? Perhaps providing educational loans, rather than grants, to aspiring college students is a sensible and more equitable public policy.

But public funding of education is not the same thing as public establishment and management of schools. Many economists believe that public control of educational institutions is the primary cause of poor educational quality in the United States, especially at the K–12 level. The reason underlying this belief is that publicly run schools do not face the constructive pressure of market competition. Public schools can perform at sub-par levels without major consequence. If schools were all privately established and operated like businesses, they would have to compete with each other for students. This competition would drive efficiency, excellence, and educational quality. To stay in business and maximize profit, each school would aspire to hire the most effective and fire the least effective instructors, provide a safe school environment, maintain high quality facilities, minimize wasteful spending, and generally do all they could do to attract students to their school.

A way to provide public funding for education, while promoting competition among schools, is through the issuance of educational vouchers. For example, a government could allocate vouchers of sufficient value to cover educational costs to all students. The vouchers could then be used to pay for entrance to the educational institution of the student's (or the student's parents') choice. Educational businesses would then compete for students. After competition runs its magic, the quality of education might just soar.

This voucher approach to education is not without implementation complications and limitations. For example, it may still be desirable for governments to establish certain educational standards that voucher receiving schools must abide by. (Should religious schools be allowed to receive taxpayer funded vouchers?) Also, the voucher strategy may not work well in rural locations where student populations may be insufficient to foster competition among schools. Ideas for dealing with these and other complications and limitations are beyond the scope of this discussion. The main lesson here is that another promising and very different approach to education exists. By harnessing the forces of competition, as has been done in so many other areas of economic life, it may be possible to revolutionize the provision of education, improve the quality of education, and create a much better educated citizenry.

90.   Drug Policy: The Case for Reducing Demand

Should the sale and use of drugs be regulated? A good economic argument for government efforts to reduce illegal drug use is that the consumption of many of these drugs can lead to negative *externalities* on society. For example, a person under the influence of an illegal drug may impose risks on others, such as may occur if the person attempts to drive. A less convincing argument is that governments need to protect people from their own poor judgment. In any case, less consumption of illegal drugs will likely benefit society.

But government programs to reduce the spread of drugs also may cause negative externalities. Such programs often fail to foresee the unintended consequences of regulation. Most notably, programs that ban or reduce the *supply* of drugs are likely to increase crime and violence! This surprising outcome may occur for at least two reasons. First, illegal drug contracts cannot be enforced through legal methods. Drug suppliers certainly can't complain to police that they have not been paid. Thus drug buyers and sellers may resort to violence as a way to enforce drug deals. Second, because illegal drugs will tend to exhibit a very *inelastic demand*, drug busts that reduce the supply of illegal drugs will drive up the price of these drugs greatly, without significantly reducing the amount of drugs that are purchased. Higher drug prices may lead to more crime by drug addicts who often must steal to obtain money to buy their drugs.

Can anything be done to reduce drug use without causing serious unintended consequences such as crime? Another policy approach offers hope. Instead of attempting to reduce the supply of drugs, the government could focus on reducing the *demand* for drugs. For example, education and counseling programs, if effective, would reduce the demand for illegal drugs. If the demand for drugs falls, drug prices will fall too. This may result in the additional benefit of less crime by drug users who steal to finance their drug habit.

What does economics have to do with drug policy? A lot.

91. Crime Policy: Deterring Crime with Incentives

People, even criminals, respond to *incentives* (see Lesson 52). Our criminal justice system uses incentives such as fines and jail time to deter crime. But how large should these incentives be and what form should they take?

A common saying is "the punishment should fit the crime." To some degree this makes sense. For example, if all criminals were caught, a $100 fine could deter $100 thefts, but at least a $1,000 fine would be required to deter $1,000 thefts. Indeed, if the fine for all thefts was $100, a criminal who stole $100 might as well steal more since no additional penalty would be imposed. Thus, to deter more serious crimes, the penalties for criminal behavior must increase with the severity of the crimes committed.

Of course, even if it were possible to catch all criminals, the cost of doing so would be prohibitive. Efforts to catch criminals (such as by hiring more police) should continue only as long as the marginal benefits (the marginal value of the crime reduced) exceed the marginal costs (for example, the salary of additional policeman). Thus, when the costs of enforcing a law are high, the benefits of thorough enforcement may not justify the costs. In such cases, many criminals may escape prosecution and punishments that "fit the crime" may be insufficient to deter crime.

For example, littering laws are very difficult to enforce. The cost to catch all violators would far exceed the benefit from eliminating litter. But this doesn't mean littering laws can't be effective. Suppose it is cost effective to catch only 1 in 100 violators and that the cost to society to clean up a violator's trash equaled $10. In this case a fine of $1,000 may be warranted. Faced with a $1,000 fine if caught, a person would choose to litter only if the benefits to them of littering exceeded their expected costs (.01 × $1,000 = $10). Thus, when enforcement is incomplete, penalties disproportionate to the crime may be necessary to cost effectively deter violations. Moreover, if this person chooses to litter, he or she will pay $10 on average in fines, which will cover society's cost to clean up the litter. Hence, society will be no worse off from the litter. Problem solved.

Why not completely ban littering by raising the penalty sufficiently high to deter all offenses? Because some littering is a good thing! Suppose the fine is set at $10,000 and for whatever reason, Tom would be willing to pay $20 to be permitted the convenience to litter. Since the expected benefit ($20) would be less than the expected cost (.01 × $10,000 = $100) to Tom, he would not choose to litter. But he would have been willing to pay more than the $10 cleanup cost to be allowed to litter. By paying say, $15 to litter, he would be better off and so would the rest of society. Similarly, speeding may be completely deterred by imposing the death penalty on anyone caught speeding. But some speeding is a good thing. Under some circumstances (such as during an emergency) the value of speeding to someone may exceed the expected social costs imposed by the speeding.

An important general lesson here is that complete bans are rarely economically *efficient*. Efficiency requires that penalties be set equal to, not greater than, the expected *externality* costs imposed by behavior. When violators are made to pay the social costs of their actions, an "efficient level of crime" will result.

But can financial incentives deter serious crime? No doubt they can to some degree, but if criminals have too little money to be taken away, financial penalties may be ineffective and other incentives such as prison time may be called for. In such cases, it may not be possible to make criminals compensate society for their behavior. Also, for very serious crimes (such as mass murder), no form and magnitude of penalty may be sufficient since the cost to a criminal of the greatest penalty that can be imposed on him or her (the death penalty?) may fall well short of the social cost of the crime. Moreover, some such criminals may act entirely irrationally and not respond to any incentives. In these cases, the benefits of preventing crime and apprehending perpetrators may be sufficiently great to justify large expenditures on police and other law enforcement services.

92. Environmental Policy: Reducing Pollution at Least Cost

The classic example of a negative *externality* is environmental pollution. When businesses pollute the air or water when producing their product, they impose external costs on society. Because the costs of pollution are not primarily borne by the polluter, profit-maximizing polluters will continue polluting despite the illness and premature death they may cause. Thus, when businesses pollute, free markets fail to lead to the most *efficient* or best outcome for society and government intervention is called for.

So why not completely ban pollution? Isn't zero pollution best? If you believe zero pollution is best, then you must be willing to give up your car, turn off your electrical appliances, and cope with the poverty that would undoubtedly result after our economy collapses. Free markets lead to too much pollution, but the costs of eliminating all pollution would far exceed the benefits.

So how should governments regulate polluters? The two well-known approaches are (1) "command and control" regulations (including complete bans), and (2) economic incentive strategies.

By far the most commonly used regulatory approach to reduce pollution in the United States is command and control regulations. These regulations require polluters either to reduce their pollutant emissions by a certain amount or employ some specified pollution control equipment. The main problem with command and control policies is that they tend to reduce pollution at high cost. Businesses, even within the same industry, may be quite different. Some businesses may be able to control their pollution easily, while it may be devastatingly costly for other businesses to reduce their pollution. One size doesn't fit all. Thus, requiring each business to use the same pollution control equipment or reduce emissions the same amount will reduce pollution, but not cost effectively. It may be much more cost effective to get relatively greater reductions from businesses that can achieve emission reductions most cheaply.

Economic incentive strategies are ways to achieve pollution reduction at less cost, or achieve more pollution reduction at the same cost. These strategies include (1) emission taxes, and (2) marketable emission permits. Taxing pollutant emissions provides an *incentive* for businesses to reduce emissions. An emission tax equal to the value of the damage caused by the emissions would make businesses pay the full social costs of their actions and lead to an efficient amount of pollution reduction. Emission taxes may reduce pollution at lower cost than command and control approaches because they provide more flexibility. Businesses that can reduce emissions cheaply will reduce more than most other businesses and pay less tax; businesses that can't reduce pollution cheaply will reduce less than most other businesses and pay more tax. A sufficiently high tax could achieve any desired total emission reduction at lowest overall control cost.

Marketable emission permits are another flexible strategy to achieve pollution reduction at lowest cost. With this strategy, polluters are allocated a specified number of emission permits, which they can then trade with one another. Businesses that can reduce emissions cheaply reduce more than required and sell their excess permits to other businesses. Businesses that can't reduce their emissions cheaply reduce less and buy permits from other businesses. Thus, a market for emission permits is formed and any specified amount of emission reduction can be achieved at lowest overall cost. This approach is currently used to reduce air pollutant emissions from utility plants in the United States.

Despite their long-time popularity among economists, economic incentive regulatory strategies to reduce pollution have been implemented only recently and sparingly in the United States. Political objections to these strategies have been high and have slowed acceptance. Businesses have opposed pollution taxes, preferring no or less burdensome regulation. Single-minded environmentalists have objected to permitting any pollution. More substantively, implementation challenges have been substantial. For example, when emissions cannot be cost effectively monitored, tax and marketable permit strategies are not feasible. In such cases, command and control may be necessary. Nevertheless, economic incentive strategies that harness market forces to fix the market failure caused by pollution offer a very promising new direction for the future of environmental policy.

93.   Traffic Policy: Can We Unclog Our Roads?

Driving a car imposes negative *externalities* on society such as pollution, road wear, accident risks, and perhaps most importantly, traffic congestion. Millions of Americans lose valuable time every day stuck in traffic. According to the Texas Transportation Institute's 2005 Urban Mobility Report, the current annual *opportunity costs* (which include the value of lost time and fuel costs) associated with traffic congestion in urban areas of the United States equal approximately $63 billion!

Too many vehicles clog our roads because roads are free to use. Drivers do not pay the full costs to society of their driving. Economists have a potential solution to this problem—road user charges.

Ideally, drivers should be charged a fee equal to the congestion and other costs they impose on others when they drive. This means adjusting the charge based on the road used, the time of day, the day of the week, etc. But is implementation of such a system viable? Wouldn't collecting tolls cause even worse traffic backups at toll plazas and gates? Technological advances have created a way around the toll gate backup problem. By using bar codes and debit cards, it is now possible to implement a system where drivers' debit cards can be automatically debited when their cars pass bar code readers located throughout a metropolitan area. A few electronic tolling systems are currently in place in the United States. For example, a privately-financed toll road opened in Orange County, California which uses electronic tolling and variable pricing (i.e., higher toll rates are charged during peak-hour drive time than during off-peak drive time).

But why have so few U.S. cities implemented road user charge systems? The political hurdles to passing a tax increase of any kind are high. Opponents typically object to road charges because they object to all government imposed charges or taxes or because road charges could make it difficult for low-income individuals to afford driving. But revenue raised from road user charges could be used to lower other taxes or to aid the poor.

Congested foreign cities, such as Singapore and London, have initiated road user charge systems. It is time for America's congested cities to do likewise.

94. Ethical Policy: Selling Body Parts, Parental Rights, and Get Out of Jail Passes

Are there some things that shouldn't be for sale? Undoubtedly there are, but economists offer surprisingly strong arguments for legalizing the sale of some things that most people believe should never be sold.

Consider human organs. It is illegal to sell or buy human organs such as kidneys, livers, and hearts in the United States. As a consequence, the *demand* for exceeds the *supply* of donated organs, shortages result, and thousands of people die every year waiting for organ replacements.

Can something be done about this tragedy? Consider the shortage of kidneys. The average wait for a kidney transplant is approximately 3 1/2 years and approximately 6,000 Americans die each year waiting. People are born with two kidneys. Usually they need only one. Why not allow people to sell one of their kidneys if they want to? Each person would weigh the health risks associated with losing a kidney with the income they could receive from the sale. They would sell a kidney only if they believed they were better off from doing so. Meanwhile, the buyer too would be better off and no one would be worse off. Some say it is unethical to sell body parts. But if you believe in promoting happiness and reducing suffering, then wouldn't keeping kidney sales illegal be unethical?

Consider parental rights. Though surrogate mothering arrangements and adoption are accepted today, selling children for profit certainly is not. There is clear reason to object to the sale of parental rights to grown children. While both the selling and buying adult may be better off, the sale would cause external effects on a third party—the child. Obviously, changing parents would be traumatic for most grown children, but what about very young children? Would they be worse off if their parental rights were sold? The answer is unclear. After all, who would be most likely to sell their infant? Answer: poor people who don't want their child. Who would be most likely to buy an infant? Answer: wealthy people who very much want children. Perhaps young children sold into wealthy and caring families would be more likely to live happier lives. If so, then infants as well as the selling and buying adults would all be better off from such sales. While the idea of selling parental rights may seem ethically preposterous, if everyone is likely to live happier lives from such sales, wouldn't it be ethically wrong to prohibit them?

Consider jail time. Should rich people be able to buy their way out of jail? Suppose Bill Gates enjoys beating people up. Instead of just keeping Bill in jail when he gets caught, suppose the law provided Bill the option to buy a get out of jail pass for $1 billion. Suppose Bill is caught beating someone up and chooses to pay the billion dollars (he has many billions to spare). The billion dollars could then be used to fully compensate the victim, provide critical funds to thousands of Americans suffering in poverty, or sent to less developed countries to save tens of thousands of lives. Everyone, including Bill, could be made better off from the sale of the pass. What about the precedent that would be set by this policy? Maybe Bill or some other billionaire would beat up more people if they knew they could buy their way out of jail? Well, why not let them? If the victim (as well as many others in need) are made better off from the billion-dollar charge for each offence (I sure would take a few hits from Bill for a billion dollars!), and if no one is made worse off, wouldn't this law set a good and ethical precedent?

In the end, economics cannot tell you what is or is not ethical. You have to judge for yourself. However, economics can provide insights for determining what policies will most likely alleviate suffering and promote happiness. If your morality is consistent with the notion of making the world a happier place (as mine is), then economic thinking and analysis can help you make ethical policy judgments.

The main economic principle to learn from this lesson is that voluntary exchange is beneficial to all people participating in the exchange. The more general principles to be remembered from this lesson are to keep an open mind, challenge conventional thought, and think instead of feel before you form your opinions.

95.   Poverty Policy: Redistributing the Pie—Would You Vote for Robin Hood?

The distribution of income and wealth is wide and widening in the United States. In the year 2000, families in the top 20% income bracket made roughly 11 times as much as families in the lowest 20% income bracket, up from less than 8 times as much in 1980. Much of this gap is driven by the enormous incomes earned by the top one percent income earners. Moreover, the distribution of wealth is much wider than the distribution of income in the United States, and the distribution of income and wealth is even wider around the world (see Lesson 82).

Should governments redistribute money from the rich to the poor? Will doing so lead to a happier world? A strong economic case can be made that taxing the rich and giving to the poor, at least to some extent, may increase overall happiness.

Consider billionaire Bill Gates and Tracy, an unemployed single mother. Suppose the government took $1,000 from Bill and gave it to Tracy. Though it may be impossible to prove, the reduction in happiness or *utility* to Bill from losing $1,000 will most likely be far less than the increase in happiness to Tracy from receiving the $1,000. We would expect this because of the principle of *diminishing marginal utility of income*. Since Bill has billions of dollars, he already has purchased most everything that provides him significant happiness. His loss of $1,000 might not even be noticed. But for Tracy, the $1,000 may mean needed food, clothing, and medical services can be purchased for her family. Thus, we should expect the transfer to increase overall happiness. Transfers from the rich to the poor also may provide an additional benefit in the form of reduced crime by reducing the difference between the haves and have-nots.

Too much redistribution, however, may lead to poverty and less happiness for everyone. For example, suppose the government regularly redistributed wealth such that everyone's wealth remained equal. Such a policy would destroy much of people's *incentive* to work. High-income workers may not work anymore if much of their income is taken away. Unemployed individuals may not look for a job if the government will transfer money to them if they stay unemployed. The result of complete redistribution would be far less work performed, far less goods and services produced, and a lower standard of living for everyone.

So what amount of redistribution would maximize the sum of everyone's happiness? If you know the answer to this, please let me and the IRS know.

96. Social Security and Medicare Policy: The Baby Boomer Time Bomb

America is aging. Americans are living longer and having fewer children. The post-World War II baby boom population is retiring, and at a relatively young age. As a consequence, the ratio of retirees to workers is rising rapidly. Social Security (the program that provides retirement, survivor, and retirement benefits) and Medicare (the program that provides health benefits to people over 65 years of age) are financed through payroll taxes (see Lesson 37). At the current tax rate, the day is coming when there will be too few people working to finance the mounting Social Security and Medicare bill (which already exceeds $500 billion annually!). When the Social Security program was initiated during the 1940's, the tax burden of one Social Security recipient was shared among 42 workers. By around the year 2030, the tax burden of one recipient of Social Security and Medicare will likely be shared between just two workers, as though every working couple will have an additional family member they will have to support.

How can the Social Security and Medicare systems be saved? The obvious policy options are to raise taxes or reduce benefits. Politicians, however, have insufficient *incentive* to enact such politically unpopular policies. They would prefer to leave these long-run problems for the next generation of politicians (and citizens) to deal with. Though the problem has been known for decades, a forthcoming Social Security and Medicare crisis nears year after year without policy action. The longer corrective action is delayed, the more painful and politically unattractive such action becomes.

Various "solutions" have been proposed to "fix" the forthcoming Social Security shortfall. One common proposal is to privatize the entire system. For example, everyone could be required to make contributions, but then each person could be allowed to invest their contributions as they wish, such as in the stock market. After retirement, each person could withdraw their accumulated savings. This approach is very different than the current system where contributions collected today are used to pay benefits to recipients today. The idea of giving people more choices (and more responsibility) has appeal. But the purpose of the Social Security program is to lessen financial risk and to ensure that retirees and others maintain a base level of income. Allowing people to risk their retirement funds in the stock market may defeat this purpose. What would society do with many millions of poor seniors if the stock market bombs? Moreover, even if a privatized system would yield greater returns (on average) for retirees, it is highly unlikely that returns would be large enough to "fix" the revenue shortfall problem.

Other proposals for "fixing" Social Security include (1) means testing benefits (so that wealthy retirees receive fewer benefits), (2) raising the cap above which Social Security taxes are not paid (so that wealthy workers pay a greater share of the costs), (3) raising the retirement age (since people are living longer), and (4) reducing the cost of living index used to increase benefits each year. But each of these reasonable proposals involves sacrifices in the form of benefit cuts or tax increases on some individuals. Thus, none of these options are politically popular. The alternative to action, however, is an insolvent Social Security system that will be incapable of fully funding a base level of income for non-wealthy elderly.

Meanwhile, health care costs in general and Medicare costs in particular are rising. Our aging population will only exacerbate this trend. Again, tax increases or benefit cuts may be necessary to maintain the Medicare program, but any such changes will be unpopular. For example, because Medicare pays for very expensive operations and other care for patients who are in any case very near death, over a quarter of all of the budget for Medicare goes to patients in their last year of life. Thus, one way to significantly reduce costs would be to limit Medicare coverage for very expensive procedures that are expected to extend life only days, weeks, or perhaps months. While reasonable, such a policy would be ethically controversial and undoubtedly politically unpopular.

So, there appears to be no painless solution to the Social Security and Medicare budget problems. However, there exists at least on approach to addressing these problems that may involve little or no U.S. taxpayer and retiree pain—immigration. By relaxing immigration limits, especially for individuals owning skills in short *supply*, an influx of taxpaying workers may be found to relieve the budget pressures caused by workforce shrinkage and our aging population. Let's hope that concerns about terrorism do not negate our desire to welcome new immigrant workers into our country.

97.   War/Defense Policy: The Cost of War, Security, and the Military Draft

In August 2004, President Bush signed off on a $417.5 billion military budget for the United States for fiscal year 2005. Additional funding to support ongoing military operations in Iraq and Afghanistan and for the Defense Department's efforts to fight terrorism will likely be authorized. Thus, year 2005 U.S. military spending will likely approach half a trillion dollars, exceed $4,000 per U.S. household, and nearly equal the entire rest of the world's military spending. While national defense may be a necessary *public good*, this level of spending incurs enormous *opportunity costs*. When resources are devoted to war and security, fewer resources are available to produce goods and services that would otherwise improve our quality of life (see Lesson 29).

In addition to the costs imposed by military operations, homeland security costs have become a significant burden for Americans. While the direct costs to the U.S. economy associated with the tragic events of 9/11/01 were relatively minor, the longer run military and homeland security costs triggered by these events have not been and will not be minor. Again, resources dedicated to security are resources that cannot be employed to raise our standard of living.

The wars in Iraq and Afghanistan and the general war on terrorism have prompted calls from politicians and commentators to reinstitute the military draft in the United States. While it may seem that a military draft would be a cost-saving way to staff the military, economics argues that the opposite would be true. People who volunteer to enter the military do so because their benefits exceed their costs of volunteering. Thus, those with high opportunity costs of entering, such as those with productive private sector jobs, will be less likely to do so. Those with low opportunity costs of entering, such as those unemployed, will be more likely to do so. In contrast, a military draft would remove many highly productive individuals from the private sector, thereby reducing output and harming the national economy. Thus, a military draft would cost the country more, not less, than would the voluntary approach to staffing the military. But what if not enough people volunteer? The solution to this problem is simple—increase military pay. Higher pay would provide an *incentive* to induce more individuals to enlist.

But isn't a military draft more fair? You judge. Is it more fair to (1) enslave young men and women to do work they do not wish to do, or (2) spread the cost of war throughout the country by raising taxes sufficiently high to pay for the military pay increases needed to induce enough people to volunteer? But what if people aren't willing to pay higher taxes to finance a war? Then perhaps the war isn't worth fighting.

98.   Budgetary Policy: Taxes, Spending, and Deficits

The first principle of economics is that we can't have everything we want. Resources are limited, tradeoffs are inevitable, and thus, choices must be made. Unfortunately, one of the first principles of politics is to pretend the first principle of economics doesn't exist. Campaigning politicians often promise to cut taxes, spend more on security, education, health care, and other programs, and simultaneously balance the budget. Once in office, these politicians fail to fulfill their unrealistic promises, often because they run *deficits* each year by spending more than their governments receive in taxes. Deficits are financed by borrowing from domestic or international sources. The fiscal year 2004 U.S. budget deficit equaled $412 billion.

The accumulation of deficits over time is a government's *debt*. At the end of 2004, the U.S. national debt equaled $7.6 trillion (that's $7,600,000,000,000) or roughly $25,000 per person in the United States! [Note, however, that $3.2 trillion of this debt was simply owed by one part of the U.S. government to another part. The remaining $4.4 trillion was owed to the public. Nearly $2 trillion of this amount was owed to foreigners].

Federal, State, and local governments each face fundamental budgetary policy questions:

(1) How much should they spend and tax?
(2) Should they balance their budget (spending = tax revenues)?
(3) How should they spend and tax?

Answers to these questions are linked. For example, how much money should be spent depends in part on how smartly the money is spent, and how much tax revenue should be raised depends in part on how wisely the tax revenue is collected. In general, additional spending should be undertaken only when the public benefits from the spending exceed the costs associated with raising taxes or borrowing to pay for the spending. Thus, the answer to the "How much?" question is very much case specific.

Many state governments must balance their budget by law. No such balanced budget requirements exist at the federal level in the United States. In theory, running deficits is sometimes good policy (see Lessons 36 and 100). But in practice, the inherent bias within our political system toward over spending and running deficits provides reason for some to believe that a national balanced budget requirement is merited.

Given governments' ability and inclination to tax and spend, how best should revenues be raised and spent? Both *efficiency* and equity considerations are important.

Most efficiently, governments should raise revenue by taxing socially undesirable activities rather than socially desirable activities, such as work. By taxing activities that generate negative *externalities*, social problems can be mitigated while revenues are being raised. For examples, taxes could be imposed on: (1) businesses based on the social costs caused by their pollution, (2) drivers based on the social costs caused by their contribution to traffic congestion, and (3) alcohol based on the social costs caused by the consumption of alcoholic drinks. But tax fairness also may be an important consideration. Society may prefer a *progressive tax*, such as the federal income tax, where a disproportionate share of the tax burden is borne by wealthier individuals. Or society may believe it is fairest to raise revenues by taxing "unearned" income, such as inheritances.

Government spending should occur only when the resulting benefits from the spending exceed the costs. Legitimate government spending includes spending for the provision of desired *public goods* such as defense, law enforcement, clean air, etc., and to promote positive externalities, such as may be achieved through spending on basic research and education. Spending to provide private goods (such as food, housing, or health care) is generally not justified on economic efficiency grounds, though society may choose to make such expenditures to aid the poor. In any case, voters should penalize politicians who overspend and ignore the first principle of economics. Spending incurs an *opportunity cost*. There is no free lunch.

99.   Long-Run Macroeconomic Policy: Raising Standards of Living over Time

The key to raising the standard of living within any country is simple—raise productivity. A nation's productivity, however, depends on the existence and combination of several key elements.

A country's wealth is determined by the value of the output of goods and services the country can produce. In the long run, the real value of a country's output [or *real gross domestic product* (RGDP)] is determined by the quantity and quality of the country's factors of production (labor, capital, and natural resources). While obtaining more labor, capital, and natural resources may result in more output or economic growth (growth in RGDP), the primary source of rising standards of living (rising RGDP per capita) has been and will be increases in *worker productivity*. More output produced per worker results in more goods and services available per consumer.

So what can be done to increase worker productivity? Investments in education and training, physical capital (such as machines, tools, computers, etc.), and research and development can all lead to greater worker productivity. All of these investments, however, do impose short-run costs that must be weighed against the long-run productivity benefits they provide.

A major factor underlying the growth of worker productivity (and our standard of living) in the United States during the past century has been advances in technology. But technological advances do not occur automatically. Such advances result when individuals have *incentives* to innovate, take risks, and invest in their future through education and research. Free markets provide these incentives. Governments too can promote technological progress by funding basic research.

Above all, governments must establish an environment that permits free markets to provide individuals with incentives to work hard, work smart, and innovate. To unleash the magic of free markets, governments must first provide political stability, national security, effective legal and criminal justice systems, a stable monetary system, and essential public goods such as environmental protection, disease control, and police. But governments also must not strangle free markets with over-regulation, over-spending, over-taxation, and restrictions on international trade. Once the environment for free markets has been established, individuals' desires for wealth and a better life will drive them to produce the goods and services that will raise standards of living for everyone.

Tragically, the basic building blocks for free markets to form and promote productivity do not exist in many of our world's less developed countries (see Lesson 82). Many of these countries are drowning in war, corruption, illiteracy, pollution, and disease. In these countries, worker productivities and standards of living remain unimaginably low.

100. Short-Run Macroeconomic Policy: Fighting Unemployment and Inflation

Macroeconomics is in the news every day. Government reports about the current rates of unemployment and inflation are often front-page news and can impact national political elections. Debates about what should be done about the serious problems of unemployment and inflation frequently are filled with misunderstandings, political agendas, and guesswork. To understand, critique, and potentially join these debates, you will need a basic understanding of the causes and possible cures of unemployment and inflation.

While a nation's production (and ultimately, consumption) of products and services is determined by the nation's productivity in the long run, in the short term swings in production are inevitable. For example, any event that lowers consumer or business confidence about the future economy (such as new worry about terrorism) could lead to a reduction in consumer or business spending. Consumers may become reluctant to buy new houses or cars if they are worried they might lose their jobs. Businesses may not expand their operations if they expect a downturn in the economy. Thus, lower expectations could lead to reduced spending, reduced income, still less spending, unemployment, less production, and ultimately recession (see Lesson 72). Eventually, market forces should drive prices and wages downward and thereby induce more sales and employment. But prices, and in particular wages, may not fully or quickly adjust because of contracts, minimum wage laws, and costs associated with changing prices. If sales fall and businesses can't lower wages, they will be forced to reduce employment and production, possibly by going out of business. This is how economies can get stuck in a recession, or worse, a depression. The Great Depression that began in the United States in 1929 led to a 25% unemployment rate, a 33% decline in the value of products and services produced (*real gross domestic product*), and a tremendous amount of misery. As unemployment rises, so does poverty, crime, divorce, and suicide.

There exists a quick fix for unemployment—governments can hire people. How can unemployment be reduced? Governments can knock buildings down (for example, by engaging in a war) and hire lots of people to rebuild them. How can unemployment be eliminated? Governments can hire half the unemployed to dig a big hole and the other half to refill the hole. Obviously, the quick fix employment strategy of government hiring may not create *productive* employment. Unless government hiring results in productive employment that generates products and services of value, standards of living will not improve.

Government policy, however, can be used to counteract swings in the economy to reduce unemployment in a more meaningful way. During an economic downturn caused by low consumer or business spending, a nation's government can implement expansionary *fiscal policy* or expansionary *monetary policy* to stimulate the economy. Expansionary fiscal policy involves increasing government spending or cutting taxes to increase consumer or business spending. Expansionary monetary policy involves actions by the *Federal Reserve* to increase the money supply to drive down interest rates and induce more spending (lower interest rates make it cheaper for consumers and businesses to borrow to spend). Thus, when spending, production, and employment are below their potential, government policy can be used to create or induce more spending in an attempt to increase employment and production back to their potential levels.

While the government may be able to provide a temporary boost to an economy, ultimately a nation's production is limited by the nation's factors of production (see Lesson 99). If an economy is already producing at or near its full capacity, spending or money supply increases may not induce production and employment increases. Instead, more money may chase the same amount of goods and cause inflation. Thus, a policy tradeoff typically exists between unemployment and inflation. While modest inflation may not be problematic, high inflation can interfere with the market system and penalize savers and lenders.

A quick fix also exists for inflation—governments can simply prohibit price increases by law. Such "wage and price controls" were tried in the United States during the 1970s by the Nixon Administration. But government price controls address the symptoms, not the root cause (too much money and spending) of inflation. As a consequence, as soon as price controls are lifted, inflation reappears, as it did in the 1970s. Most importantly, price controls interfere with the market system. Inevitably, shortages result for goods that experience supply reductions or demand increases if prices are not allowed to rise. Thus, this quick fix approach to fighting inflation is likely to cause more harm than good.

Alternatively, government policy makers can counteract inflation by using contractionary fiscal or monetary policy (by lowering government spending, raising taxes, or decreasing the money supply). *Federal Reserve* action to contract the money supply and reduce consumer and business spending has been the U.S. government's most frequently used policy tool to prevent or fight inflation (see Lesson 38).

Unfortunately, the use of fiscal and monetary policy to stabilize economies and fight unemployment and inflation has serious limitations. In particular, a great amount of uncertainty always exists regarding the best size and timing of fiscal and monetary policy actions. These policies take a long time to implement and impact the economy. For example, by the time the U.S. Congress recognizes the economy is in a recession, passes an expansionary budget that is approved by the President, implements spending increases and tax cuts, and the effect of these actions trickles through the economy, the recession could be long over and the expansionary policy may cause inflation. Indeed, some economists believe attempts to stabilize the economy using active fiscal and monetary policy are likely to cause more instability. Most economists believe governments should not attempt to fine tune the economy, but that they should instead apply the tools of fiscal and monetary policy only when the economy gets substantially off track.

101. International Trade Policy: Many Winners and a Few Losers

Imagine a law that prohibited trade. Such a law would require you to produce every product or service you want to consume. You may be a great economics teacher, but if you don't know how to build a house, don't own land to grow food, and don't have a source of energy to keep you warm in the winter, you may not be able to survive. Now suppose the law permitted trade, but just within your neighborhood. Perhaps now you could trade your time and advice with your neighbors in exchange for essentials. You may now be able to survive, but your life (and your neighbors' lives) would be poor. Now suppose the law permitted trade, but only within your country. If you live in Maryland, you could sell your teaching services to earn money to buy potatoes from Idaho, wine from California, oranges from Florida, automobiles from Michigan, and ski vacations from Colorado. The opportunity to trade with anyone within the United States would greatly improve the quality of your life. This fact is not controversial. But if expanding trade throughout the United States improves standards of living, wouldn't expanding trade throughout the world raise standards of living further? The answer is yes, it would. Nevertheless, international trade and the "globalization" of our economy remain very controversial issues.

Nearly all economists agree that trade among nations makes all trading nations richer. Trade is like a magic invention. A handshake can convert Iowa wheat into French wine, a Japanese car, or Swiss watches. Even when a poor country can't produce anything as efficiently as a rich country, both countries can benefit from trading with each other. For example, even if U.S. workers can produce shirts more quickly than Mexican workers (because they may be higher skilled and have access to better machinery), it still may make sense for the United States to import shirts from Mexico. Importing clothing frees time and resources allowing the United States to produce and export other products and services that they can produce even more efficiently (at a lower *opportunity cost*). When countries specialize in the production of products and services they have *comparative advantage* in producing and then trade with each other, both countries can end up with more of all goods traded.

Plenty of real world evidence supports the economists' theoretical arguments for free trade. For example, the most isolated countries, such as North Korea, remain desperately poor. Meanwhile China and Southeast Asia have experienced rapid economic growth in large part because of expanding trade with the rest of the world. As for the United States, international economists Gary Clyde Hufbauer and Paul L.E. Grieco estimated that the increase in U.S. trade with other countries over the last half century has led to an increase in U.S. income of roughly $1 trillion (or on average, $10,000 per household) annually. Moreover, these researchers estimated that movement from today's mostly free trade world to a completely free trade world would generate an additional $500 billion (or on average, $5,000 per household) annually for U.S. citizens. Thus, empirical evidence indicates the benefits of free international trade may be quite large.

So why do some people protest against global trade and lobby politicians to enact protectionist policies such as import *tariffs* and *quotas*? The primary reasons underlying this behavior are self-interest and ignorance. It is easy to understand that some people are harmed by international trade. The unrestricted importation of inexpensive textiles into the United States from Mexico may provide substantial cost savings for U.S. consumers, a way out of poverty for Mexican workers (see Lesson 34), and long-run employment increases in the United States (see Lesson 32). [It also may avoid retaliatory tariffs, quotas, or other protectionist policies that Mexico could impose on various U.S. industries that export to Mexico.] But clearly, textile workers in North Carolina are made worse off from these imports. The costs of international trade are concentrated and obvious, whereas the benefits are widespread and less obvious. Thus, industry interest groups are often successful in their efforts to organize and lobby politicians to protect their industry from foreign competition, despite the greater good that would result from free international trade (see Lesson 61).

The bottom line: International trade results in many winners and a few losers; protectionist policies result in many losers and a few winners. Unfortunately, the few sometimes have more influence on public policy than the many.

ECONOMICS FOR LIFE:
FINAL THOUGHTS AND NEXT STEPS

With 101 lessons behind you, you should understand that economics is everywhere and applies to everything. It is at your school, within your home, at your work, in your news, throughout your neighborhood, and around your world. But mostly, economics is within your mind. Economic reasoning can help you think, understand, and decide.

But economics provides few answers by itself. It serves to help you think, understand, and decide, but rarely tells you what to think and do. To decide what to think and do, you should apply economics to the particular situations or problems you face in life in light of your personal preferences and goals. If you become comfortable thinking like an economist, you will be able to apply the lessons of economics not just to 101 problems, but to thousands of real world situations you will encounter throughout your life.

Your next steps are your choice. Your opportunities for applying the lessons of economics are never-ending. But remember,

The real purpose of education is <u>not</u> knowledge. The real purpose of education is action!

I offer you a few prospects for action:

(1) Review the summary of the most important general lessons from economics listed in Appendix A3.

(2) Think and act like an economist to reduce waste, avoid decision-making mistakes, and make yourself and your family better off. Make better decisions by carefully and comprehensively weighing the marginal benefits and costs of: (1) financial decisions about what to buy and how to invest and, (2) personal decisions by about how you spend your time and effort.

(3) Assess the business you work for to identify ways to increase efficiency and profitability. Apply marginal

thinking to production and hiring decisions. Identify pricing strategies that might increase profits in light of your competition.

(4) Tune in to, see, and enjoy the world around you. Become an "economic naturalist" by observing, understanding, and predicting individual and market behavior using your knowledge of economics and the incentives facing people.

(5) Read, listen, and watch the news with a new critical eye. See past the obvious, around the biased, and through the inaccurate. Consider the incentives facing politicians and the media when they speak to you. Anticipate the usually unanticipated consequences of government actions.

(6) Talk about economic ideas and issues with your friends and family. Teach them what you have learned. Teach others about the poverty, illness, and suffering that is still widespread around the world. Inspire others to act with you.

(7) Be politically active: vote, volunteer, lobby, or run for office. Hold politicians accountable when they put politics ahead of good economics.

(8) Learn more about economics. Learn and apply much more than the 101 lessons in this book. Read popular, thought provoking economics books such as *Hidden Order* by David Friedman, *Armchair Economist* by Steven Landsburg, and *Naked Economics* by Charles Wheelan (I recommend you read Wheelan's book first). Read newspapers, news websites, and news magazines to learn about current economic conditions and events. Take advanced classes and major in economics if you are so inclined. Learn and use what you learn to help yourself and others.

Best of luck

APPENDICES

A.1   101 LESSONS LINKED TO HOUGTON-MIFFLIN ECONOMIC PRINCIPLES TEXTBOOKS

Topics	Madariaga *Economics for Life* Lessons	Boyes/Melvin *Economics*[1] Chapters	Boyes/Melvin *Fundamentals of Economics*[2] Chapters	Taylor *Economics*[3] Chapters
Key Concepts: Scarcity, Opportunity Cost, Comparative Advantage	1, 3, 7, 10, 12–13, 15–17, 20, 22, 29, 32, 46–47, 54–58, 68, 93, 97–98, 101	1–2	1	1
Supply and Demand	4, 11, 48-50, 59, 66-67, 69–70, 79, 84, 90, 94	3	2–3	3
Unemployment and Inflation	10, 30–33, 41, 63, 71–72, 100	8	11	17
Fiscal Policy/ Deficits/Debt	10, 29, 35–36, 38, 98, 100	12	13	26
Money and Monetary Policy	7, 10, 26, 38–40, 71, 100	13–14	14–15	22, 27
Economic Growth/ Tech. Progress	30, 48, 54, 64, 82, 99	17-18	16	21, 28
International Trade	32–35, 101	19, 35–36	17–18	29, 30
Elasticity	6, 20, 24, 44, 50, 69–70, 73–74, 90	20	4	4
Consumer Choices	1–2, 5–11	21	—	5
Costs of Production	17–18, 23, 25, 45, 64	22	5	8
Profits/Profit Maximization	17–20, 23–25	23	5	9
Monopoly Power/ Price Discrimination	6, 18, 20, 45, 64, 73–74	25	4, 6	10
Labor Markets	4, 14, 21–22, 59, 67, 80, 83	30	—	13
Redistribution/Poverty/Social Security	28, 37, 82, 95–96	33–34	8	14
Market Failures/ Gov't Policy / Gov't Failure	25, 56, 60–62, 81–82, 86–93, 98, 100	28	8	15
Financial Markets	10–11, 51	31	—	16

[1]Sixth edition, [2]Third edition, [3]Fifth edition

A.2   101 LESSONS LINKED TO SPECIFIC ECONOMIC CONCEPTS

This appendix links specific economic concepts taught in economic principles classes to the lessons within *Economics of Life* where these concepts are applied. When learning these concepts, students may want to consult this appendix to identify applications that illustrate how these concepts can be used to make decisions or to better understand the world. When teaching these concepts, instructors may wish to consult this appendix to identify interesting and relevant applications for use within your lectures, to motivate classroom discussion, and/or to assign as homework reading.

Lessons Illustrating Specific Economic Concepts

Capitalism/Free Markets: Lessons 62, 81–82, 84, 89, 94

Common Property Problem: Lesson 65

Comparative Advantage: Lessons 12, 22, 32, 68, 101

Crowding Out: Lessons 29, 36

Debt/Deficits: Lessons 10, 35–36, 38, 98

Diminishing Marginal Utility: Lessons 20, 27, 83, 95

Diminishing Returns: Lessons 15–16, 19

Discounting: Lessons 1, 17

Efficiency: Lessons 84, 91-92, 98

Elasticity: Lessons 6, 20, 24, 44, 50, 69, 70, 73–74, 90

Externalities: Lessons 25, 56, 86, 89–93, 98

Economic Profit: Lessons 17, 20, 25

Economies of Scale: Lessons 18, 45, 64, 88

Fallacy of Composition: Lessons 69, 71–72, 75–76

Fiscal Policy: Lessons 29, 38, 100

Government Failure: Lessons 61–62, 81–82, 87–88

Incentives/Behavior: Lessons 7-8, 13, 22, 45, 48–49, 52–54, 57–59, 61–62, 65, 77–78, 81–82, 84, 86, 91–92, 95–96

Incomplete Information: Lessons 2, 6, 8, 14, 21–22, 55, 86

Inflation: Lessons 10, 41, 63, 71, 100

International Trade/Protectionism: Lessons 32–35, 61, 101

Marginal Thinking: Lessons 1–2, 15–16, 19, 21, 23–24, 66, 91

Market Structures/Profit Maximization: Lessons 18–20, 24

Monetary Policy/Federal Reserve: Lessons 7, 38, 40, 71, 100

Money: Lessons 10, 26, 39, 40

Monopoly/Monopoly Power: Lessons 18–19, 20, 24, 45, 64, 86

Opportunity Cost/Scarcity/Tradeoffs: Lessons 1, 3, 7, 10, 12–13, 15–17, 20, 29, 46–47, 54-58, 93, 97–98

Poverty: Lessons 28, 82, 95

Price Discrimination: Lessons 6, 20, 73–74

Prisoner's Dilemma Problems: Lessons 21, 24, 75–76

Public/Non-Rival Goods: Lessons 12, 86, 98

Recession: Lessons 10, 72, 100

Real vs. Nominal Values: Lessons 5, 10, 41, 63–64, 71

Regulation/Unintended Consequences: Lessons 44, 46, 77–80, 85, 88, 100

Social Security: Lessons 37, 96

Sunk Costs: Lessons 15, 25

Supply and Demand: Lessons 4, 11, 18, 48–50, 59, 66–67, 69–70, 79, 84, 90, 94

Technological Progress: Lessons 30, 48, 54, 64

Unemployment: Lessons 10, 30–33, 72, 100

A.3   101 LESSONS LINKED TO KEY GENERAL
        ECONOMIC LESSONS

This appendix links the most important general lessons from economics to the lessons within *Economics for Life* where these general lessons are illustrated. To obtain a summary of the main lessons from economics (and the main lessons from *Economics for Life*), students should carefully review this appendix. Instructors may wish to consult this appendix to identify specific illustrations of the general economic lessons below for use within your lectures, to motivate classroom discussion, and/or to assign as homework reading.

ABOUT DECISION MAKING:

- **We Can't Have Everything We Want—***Scarcity* **Requires Us to Make Choices that Involve** *Tradeoffs*

  Lessons 10, 15–16, 46–47, 97–98

- **Decisions Should be Made by Comparing** *Marginal Benefits* **with** *Marginal Costs*

  Lessons 1–2, 15–16, 19, 21, 23–24, 66, 91

- **All** *Opportunity Costs* **Should Be Identified and Considered When Making Decisions and When Trying to Understand and Predict Others' Decisions**

  Lessons 1, 3, 7, 10, 12–13, 15–17, 20, 29, 46–47, 54–58, 93, 97–98

- *Incentives Drive Behavior* **by Affecting the Benefits and Costs of Decisions—Behavior Can Be Understood and Predicted by Identifying the Incentives People Face and Changed by Altering the Incentives People Face**

  Lessons 7–8, 13, 22, 45, 48–49, 52–54, 57–59, 61–62, 65, 77–78, 81–82, 84, 86, 91–92, 95–96

- It Is the *Real Value* or Purchasing Power of Money that *Matters* When Making Financial Decisions

  Lessons 5, 10, 41, 63–64, 71

- *Happiness* Depends on Much *More than* Financial *Wealth*—Your Decisions in Life Should Reflect Recognition of This Fact

  Lessons 26–27, 64, 83

ABOUT OUR ECONOMIC SYSTEM AND THE ROLE OF GOVERNMENT:

- The Forces of *Supply and Demand* Determine the *Prices and Quantities* of Everything Bought and Sold

  Lessons 4, 11, 18, 48–50, 59, 66–67, 69–70, 79, 84, 90, 94

- Free Market *Capitalism* with Private Ownership of Property, Unrestricted and Voluntary Exchange, and Competition Among Sellers and Among Buyers, *Generates Wealth*

  Lessons 62, 81–82, 84, 89, 94

- *Free Markets* Sometimes *Fail*—Government Corrections of Market Failures Can Improve Social Well-Being

  Lessons 86, 89–93, 95, 98, 100

- *Governments* Sometimes *Fail*—Public Agencies May Not Face Competitive Pressure to Excel, Regulation May Result in Unintended Consequences, and the Interests of Politicians and Bureaucrats May Not Align with the Interests of Society

  Lessons 44, 46, 61–62, 77–82, 85, 87–88, 100

ABOUT ECONOMY-WIDE ISSUES:

- **Too Much Money and Spending Can Cause *Inflation*; Too Little Money and Spending Can Cause *Unemployment*—Policy Makers Can Affect the Money Supply and Spending through *Monetary and Fiscal Policies***

  Lessons 10, 41, 63, 71–72, 100

- **Advancing *Technology and Worker Productivity* are the Keys to Raising *Standards of Living* Over Time—Providing Incentives for People to Innovate, Work Hard, and Invest, Is the Key to Advancing Technology and Worker Productivity**

  Lessons 64, 99

- **Countries Gain By *Specializing* in What They Do Relatively Best and *Freely Trading* with Other Countries**

  Lessons 32–33, 101

- **Most of the World's Countries and *People Remain Very Poor***

  Lessons 28, 34, 82, 95, 99